DON'T JUST SURVIVE,
THRIVE

DON'T JUST SURVIVE, THRIVE

A Teacher's Guide to Fostering Resilience, Preventing Burnout, and Nurturing Your Love for Teaching

SARAJANE HERRBOLDT
illustrated by KAY WATERSON

Published by:
ULYSSES PRESS
PO Box 3440
Berkeley, CA 94703
www.ulyssespress.com

ISBN: 978-1-64604-082-7
Library of Congress Control Number: 2020935670

Printed in the United States
10 9 8 7 6 5 4 3 2 1

Acquisitions editor: Casie Vogel
Managing editor: Claire Chun
Editor: Debra Riegert
Proofreader: Renee Rutledge
Front cover design: fiverr
Artwork: Kay Waterson except quote backgrounds on pages 21, 32, 96, 168, 187 © chyworks/shutterstock.com
Interior design: Jake Flaherty

CONTENTS

INTRODUCTION

Throughout my career in education, I've encountered a lot of incredible human beings doing the good, important, and hard work of educating. Some of these individuals stood out as exceptional, so I started to ask what set them apart from the rest and what kept them committed to the profession. I soon realized that the answers to these questions are not necessarily one and the same.

This book is written from both my personal and professional experience. Shortly before I began my career, I imagined the celebration and praise that would come from the commitment and longevity I would offer students and schools. Never did I anticipate that my final years working within a school would become some of the most painful to navigate.

During my last year, I encountered not one, not two, but three people who had to take a leave of absence due to high levels of workplace stress and its impact on their health and well-being. I didn't work with a large staff. These were individuals I cared for and shared day-to-day interactions with on a regular basis. In the course of one year, they were pushed to their limits over and over again and reached what felt like a breaking point. I felt so limited in what I could do to support them. No changes made to the educational system were significant enough to sustain them doing the work. Instead, the necessary relief came from stepping away from their job for the time being, and for some of them, permanently.

I continue to hear from many other educators who find themselves at the end of their rope. Many feel as though they are on the verge of something that feels more uncomfortable than comfortable. That shouldn't be the way we support our educators.

The Problem: Burnout

It is a commonly known fact that 30 to 50 percent of educators leave the profession within their first five years of teaching due to workplace stress and burnout. While this is not a recent discovery, we have done little to shift how we approach the problem. The word "burnout" is thrown around a lot, but it is not always taken seriously. Perhaps that is because we tend to view it as an individual problem rather than a community problem.

We also know that students show up in our classrooms with more than just academic needs that we as educators often feel obligated to address. Oftentimes, these needs are connected to a struggle or trauma that a student is encountering. When we intentionally put ourselves in close proximity to another individual's struggle and trauma, we run the risk of experiencing some trauma ourselves. We must begin to have honest conversations with ourselves, our colleagues, our administrators, school boards, and lawmakers to address how workplace stress and burnout impact educators. If we do not begin to have such conversations, we may soon experience a crisis due to a shortage of educators who are willing to work in such demanding conditions.

Without caring, committed, professional educators, who will facilitate the learning of the next generation?

Much like we want to safeguard children from the many potential harms of the world that bring danger, pain, and grief, we need to consider what it might look like to offer ourselves a similar practice of safeguarding. Can we protect children from every potential harm? Unfortunately, we cannot. Can we guarantee that our adult life will be absent of disappointments, challenges, and stress? Absolutely not. However, what we can give children and ourselves is the courage to face a challenge and move through it with coping strategies that help us repair, recover, and perhaps even improve.

How Do We Not Just Survive, but Thrive?

When I encounter a new challenging situation, I am eager to discover and learn any applicable content I can to help me resolve the problem. I "jump into the deep end," and my passion grows as I continue to learn. I want to take it all in and find a workable solution as quickly possible. However, time and time again, I get busy and then my attention grows fragmented. I become overwhelmed or shift back into old habits of being and thinking. When that sense of urgency creeps up again, I repeat this pattern and somehow expect a different outcome. Is this familiar to anyone else?

Over the years, after a lot of reflection and failed attempts, I realized that if I wanted a different outcome, I needed to respond in a different way. Rather than trying to make all of the mental, emotional, and physical lifestyle changes at one time, I needed to be more deliberate and intentional with an ongoing daily practice of shifting the little things. The change I was seeking for myself was less about a one-and-done situation. Instead, subtle shifts and a sustained intentional effort would bring about greater change and help me broaden my capacity to be resilient and deepen my overall sense of well-being.

What would it look like to be proactive rather than reactive in our day-to-day lives and throughout the course of a school year? What would it look like to support educators and their well-being before they reached a tipping point that potentially led to their breaking point? What would it look like to allow teachers to take a sabbatical, similar to other professions, to help them recharge, rejuvenate, and learn without being overwhelmed?

By no means do I hold all the answers or have the magic solution to make it right or better. Disappointing, I know. But just like you, I am an educator. My work as an educator has been some of the most rewarding *and* challenging work I've ever done. I've been a classroom teacher for students in preschool through 2nd grade, and have provided support services to students spanning kindergarten through 12th grade, in my work as a district coordinator. I have spent plenty of time fretting over whether or not my lesson plans were good enough and met all the necessary requirements, or if my students felt connected enough to engage in learning. I continually worried about whether or not I could get it all done. I did not want to fall short and let down my students, their families, or my colleagues. I often questioned how much time was an acceptable amount to take away from my own children and partner in order to make my instruction better. I wondered if I was alone in fretting about these things and continually thinking I wasn't doing enough. So, I started to dive into research surrounding the field of education. I wondered what the life of a teacher might look like if we reimagined the way we support our educators so they could feel as though they were thriving instead of simply surviving.

I've experienced many beautiful and challenging moments as an educator. I realized that I could either keep these moments to myself so that no one would know the details of my journey, or I could share them. I decided (and here lies my deep, heartfelt desire from what I have come to believe and know) that sharing my experiences with others who were on a similar journey would make us feel a little less lonely. So often in education, we end up working alone with little time to connect to ourselves and others throughout the day. I believe we are better together. When we feel connected, we experience a stronger sense of belonging and find the courage to trust and be vulnerable with not only each other, but ourselves as well.

"While you're living ... all you can do is have passion. ...You write in order to change the world, knowing perfectly well you probably can't.... The world changes according to the way people see it, and if you alter, even by a millimeter, the way a person looks or people look at reality, then you can change it."

—James Baldwin

YOU ARE DOING THE GOOD, IMPORTANT, HARD WORK!

Each time I sat down to write, I thought of you, dear reader, and the multitude of things I wanted to share with you. It remains my hope that even when the words feel difficult to absorb, you eventually find the comfort that allows you to reconnect, reprioritize, and reflect on you. This is not the first book to highlight the topic of educators and their stress, or address the topic of resilience. I am hopeful that it won't be the last either, because echoes of a message often amplify its importance.

This book addresses the multiple complexities educators must learn in order to navigate how trauma impacts more than just our students, and how we benefit from practices that promote resilience. Each section provides a variety of interactive ideas and activities to consider. You may want to read this book straight through, or set it down and come back to it again and again throughout the school year.

There is some overlap between each of the sections because each topic is quite robust in and of itself. To piecemeal the learning offered within each section diminishes the interconnectedness of the topics and inhibits the cyclical nature of the work. This book does not provide a quick fix or a one-size-fits-all solution. Instead, I encourage you to seek out the information that speaks to you to help you build your capacity to recover from the daily stressors and struggles and move forward, otherwise known as resilience, so that you can continue doing the good, important, hard work of being an educator.

My hope is that the information and practices regarding educators, trauma, and resilience provided in this book encourages you to dive fearlessly into your own well-being. Maybe it will also bring some momentum toward solving this national problem of teacher sustainability by supporting educators to thrive rather than just survive. So, grab a pen or pencil and underline, circle, mark up, record, or reflect on whatever resonates with you. Notice the emotions that rise up for you while reading, reflecting, or practicing. Check in with yourself to help deepen your understanding of who you are. Use the information provided to help you speak your truth, reflect on your own story, and invest in yourself. It's okay for you to pour a little bit, or even a lot, back into yourself so you can keep offering all of your goodness back to others.

Finally, I believe in amplifying voices as much as possible. I also believe in the power of personal stories and the learning that can happen when we take time to listen to others. This is not a struggle unique to me so it felt important to allow others to share their journeys as well. As my awareness and practices started to shift toward prioritizing my resilience and well-being, I began to ask others about their journey as an educator. Specifically, what led them to a career in education, and what keeps them there? What advice would they give a new teacher, and what other roles do they find themselves filling? What are some of the rewards and challenges they have encountered over the course of their career? Do they identify themselves as a resilient educator? Throughout the following pages, you will find some of those personal stories from a handful of other educators. You will read about their passion, their love for children, their tenacity, their struggle and pain, and their resilience. Perhaps you will even find echoes of yourself reflected within their words. I certainly hope you do.

Throughout our lifetimes, we will all stumble. In fact, no one is immune to struggle. We will all encounter it and feel a sense of unsteadiness at some point. My hope is that when you do encounter these moments, you can look around and know you are not alone. If you make space for it, you will find your footing again. If I could walk alongside you on this journey, I would. Everyone deserves a companion, even on the most difficult and windiest of roads, to help them feel steady and to encourage and empower them throughout the journey. I have to believe that we can hold onto hope and see how small changes can lead to a big impact, and perhaps lead to a ripple effect that benefits not just one, but many, and then hopefully impacts the system as a whole. Until then, may these pages be your companion and offer you clarity, encouragement, and hope, and bring you a little further along on your journey. Now, breathe deep and hold on, dear reader, because together we are so much better than alone.

DON'T JUST SURVIVE. **THRIVE**

PART I
The State of Education

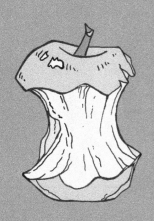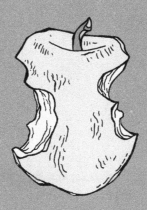

CHAPTER 1

WHY DID YOU BECOME AN EDUCATOR?

Raise your hand if you know an educator.

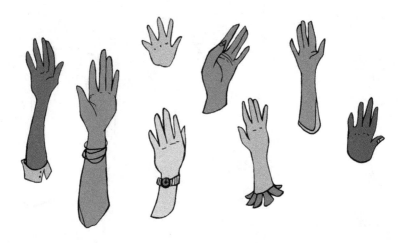

Think of the teachers you read about as a child. I'm sure we can all picture at least one. Consider, for example, Miss Eva Beadle from *Little House on the Prairie*, Miss Frizzle from *The Magic School Bus*, Professors Dumbledore and McGonagall from Harry Potter, John Keating from *Dead Poets Society,* or Mr. Holland from *Mr. Holland's Opus*. These characters were passionate educators who devoted their lives to teaching essentials like reading, writing, and arithmetic. They maintained a sense of order while cultivating meaningful relationships with their students, even those who were the most challenging and unruly of learners, and impacting their lives in a significant way. They often sat in front of a big wooden desk on which piles of books, cups full of sharpened pencils, and if they were lucky enough, an apple sat as a sign of appreciation and admiration.

This simplistic notion of teaching and my deeply rooted desire to help others (and let's be honest, my love for school supplies and organizing), led me to pursue a career in education.

I encourage you to think about what led you to a career in education. Was it the love for school supplies? Who doesn't love a new pen, notebook, or fresh stack of Post-it notes? Perhaps it was the allure of having time off with no work during one of the most enjoyable seasons of the year. Maybe it was your desire to cultivate curiosity or to connect with students in meaningful ways and see them grow and thrive over the course of the day or school year. My guess is you didn't pursue this career for the money. So, why exactly did you seek a career in education? The following personal account may help you recall the answer.

> "Stay grounded
> in your why."
> —Colleen W., educator

A Personal Account of Building Resilience

by Emily C., secondary language arts teacher

As a secondary English language arts teacher, I am often asked, "Did you always know you wanted to be a teacher?" While many of my colleagues (and I'm sure many of yours, too) have grand stories of their mothers and grandmothers being teachers, that just wasn't my reality. Instead, my father sells motors, my mother is a merchandiser, both of my grandfathers were in the auto industry, my maternal grandmother was a nurse, and my paternal grandmother was a secretary. Teaching was about as far from my radar as Pluto. So, the answer is no, I did not always know I wanted to be a teacher. But every sign along the way pointed me to a career in the classroom.

Like many young people, I had no idea what I wanted to do when I grew up. In the 3rd grade I was absolutely positive I would be an author who would write grandiose stories for children. By 4th grade, I was convinced becoming a fashion designer would be the best job ever. In the 5th grade I was determined to be the first female to make it to the NFL. Like many kids, my career path was all over the place. While in middle school, I was told by my teachers that I needed to start considering my future a bit more. So, I got out a notebook and started listing ideas. These ideas ranged from a lawyer (large part in thanks to my mom suggesting it since I always managed to "argue the taste of air" with anyone who would let me) to a physical therapist (due to the soccer injuries and subsequent surgeries and physical therapy I endured) and just about every possible thing in between. I had big ideas, but no real direction.

I gave up on becoming a lawyer pretty quickly, but the physical therapist notion stuck with me until my sophomore year of high school. It was during this year that I was given the opportunity to dissect a fetal pig in my biology class. While this was a very cool unit and I learned a lot, this exercise convinced me to rule out anything involving the medical field. Also, I came to the realization that I cannot see others in pain. I am far too empathetic. I spent the next year sort of lost in terms of a career direction. There wasn't necessarily anything that I was particularly good at, or that I knew I would enjoy doing.

During the summer following my junior year of high school, I was hired by Wendy's. It took only a week for me to realize I was not cut out for making sandwiches. My manager sat me down and kindly said, "Emily, I just don't think this is going to work." After spending some time wallowing and figuring I was destined to be a failure for the rest of my life, I went back to the notebook I wrote in when I was 11 years old. I crossed out some of the ideas I knew weren't right for me. Out went NFL player, astronaut, and nurse. I whittled down the list until I was left with two options going into my senior year that I felt I could be good at: social work or teaching. I had always loved serving others and working with kids. These two professions seemed to cater to what I loved.

As a high school senior I was able to spend two class periods a day working as a teacher's aide at my former middle school and attend a local university to start earning some college credits. This allowed me to really do some soul searching and figure out what I wanted from life. While attending the university, I took a social work class on grief and loss. Shortly after that class began, I realized I was not cut out to be a social worker—flashback to the whole *I'm too empathetic* thing. That left teaching as my other option. I absolutely loved the work, from grading papers, recording grades, and working in small groups with those who were struggling to simply being in the classroom and around students. I simply fell in love; there was no turning back for me.

Looking back, I have very vivid memories of silently critiquing teachers' lessons or classroom layouts or specific assignments—not that I knew anything at the time about teaching, but I remember thinking *if only they did it this way instead*. I can remember being a 1st-grade student and being placed in a group with another student who wasn't quite getting his sight words. As I was always a very strong reader, I took it upon myself to create worksheets centered around his sight words. I gave them to him, and we reviewed the answers at recess.

I am writing this account the summer following my first year as a lead classroom teacher. I spent the weeks following that last day of the school year reflecting. The 2019–2020 school year held some major events for me personally, my school community as a whole, and even the world. At the start of the year, we lost a student to suicide. I started an after-school calligraphy club. My boyfriend and I spent the year long distance as we realized we wanted to move forward with our relationship. I was given an opportunity to coach our girls' soccer team. I lost a friend from college to suicide. Just as I was starting to feel like I had my groove and my classroom was feeling like mine, schools shut down due to a global pandemic, and teaching and learning shifted to the virtual realm.

Even with all of this year's curveballs, I have grown more and more confident that teaching is the right profession for me. Looking back at all of the small instances in which I thought *what the heck am I supposed to do now?*, I am proud of how I handled situations I had never even fathomed I would need to navigate. I found ways to stay connected with my students through the midst of distance learning—some of whom are still continuing to reach out to me even after school has ended. *I may not always feel like I know exactly what to do in the moment, but somehow my gut leads me in the right direction.* Even though I don't come from a teaching family, teaching is and will always be in my blood.

What Led You to a Career in Education?

Can you remember the "why" that led you to a career in education? Don't worry, there are no wrong answers here. Our "why" typically grows out of, and remains connected to, our values, which continue to guide and move us forward. If you, as a preservice educator, had written down your "why," would it still hold true for you today? Is it still connected to the work you are doing?

Knowing your "why" is something that you will come back to again and again over the course of your career. When we find the alignment to our "why," it leaves us standing tall and smiling from ear to ear. It is also the thing we question during the most challenging of days as we wonder if it is even an attainable possibility.

I invite you to spend a few minutes thinking about your "why." Then grab your favorite pen or pencil and write it down to help you gain even greater awareness and clarity. It may take a few words or a few pages to summarize it, but once you've identified it, consider hanging it somewhere in your classroom as a reminder, and come back to it throughout your career.

What Is Your Why?

_____

_____

_____

_____

_____

What Is Your Why? (continued)

DON'T JUST SURVIVE, **THRIVE**

CHAPTER 2

FOR THE LOVE OF LEARNING

Many teach for their love of learning or a desire to help others. As a student, I was fortunate to have teachers who instilled in me a love of learning. Even to this day, I find that I can't quite satisfy that feeling of having learned enough. I am always eager to deepen my understanding of a topic and learn more. I also had teachers who created an environment that felt safe and predictable, which ultimately felt like a place where I could take risks.

Several teachers, in particular, stand out for me. As they come to mind, I realize that they are all educators who helped me navigate some of my most challenging moments of childhood and early adulthood. They bore witness to some of my greatest moments of pain and some of the most pivotal moments in my life. In 1st grade, Ms. Rich let me stay in during afternoon recess and "file papers" because I was overwhelmed with having just moved to a new town. Mrs. Bertalot, my 2nd-grade teacher, knew some of the pain I was experiencing and let me be that quiet, shy girl who sat in the back corner by the windows. When she found me sitting and staring out the window for a little too long, she gently pulled my attention back to what was happening within the classroom. On the last day of school, she loaded up my backpack with extra handwriting books to fill my upcoming and unstructured days of summer, and reminded me that I was a good person. Ms. Kaiser, my 7th-grade English teacher, began each class with journal writing. On the days when time was up and I was still furiously scribing away, she let me continue a bit longer. If I asked her to comment on my writing, she always returned it the very next day with a response that was connected to the words I had shared. In high school, my band teacher, Mr. Bray, had an open office policy and allowed students to visit and share their life experiences. He demonstrated the importance of listening and gently guiding. He also cultivated in me the ability to be a leader, while also learning to not limit myself regardless of my current circumstance or what may lay ahead. These are just a few examples of the ways in which my teachers played a part in creating safety in order to help cultivate my learning.

Who Were Your Influential Teachers?

Reflect on your time in school and some of your favorite teachers. Think about the culture they created within their classrooms. What stands out to you? What decisions did they make that helped you feel safe and secure in their classroom so you could take risks and keep on learning? Who encouraged and inspired you along the way, and how was this done? Do you think that the teachers who were your role models influence who you are now as an educator?

Pick up the favorite pen or pencil again, and feel free to jot some names and memories here.

What changed from the days of being inspired by those educators to now?

_____

_____

_____

_____

_____

_____

_____

_____

_____

CHAPTER 3

STRESSED-OUT EDUCATORS

"This is one of the hardest jobs you will ever have. Be ready to sacrifice. Be ready to be exhausted. Be ready to take it all home with you: the work, the books, the papers to grade, the emotions, the worry, and the stress. All of it."

—Edna T., educator

Raise your hand if you know a stressed-out educator.

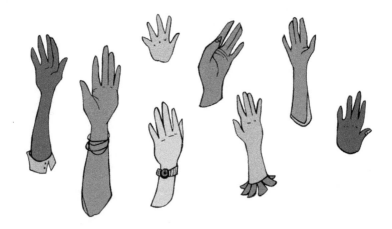

How many stressed-out educators do you know? Are you one of them? Teaching is a career choice of service that requires constant change for little money. It is an incredibly rewarding but demanding profession that requires you to have a high level of tolerance for multiple things in order to get through the day.

During a study conducted between 1985 and 2012, the number of teachers over the course of a 27-year span of time experiencing high stress during their work week increased from 35 percent to 51 percent.[1] You read that right, 51 percent!

According to the American Institute of Stress, teachers are more likely to suffer job-related stress than other professionals.[2] I recently had the opportunity to present at a conference for trauma-sensitive schools. On the final day of the conference, the keynote speaker stated that educators rank high on the list for job-related stress, no surprise there. In fact, educators come in second place after nurses who work in emergency rooms. I don't know the veracity of this statement, and I have yet to find the research to confirm it, but I wouldn't be surprised if it was the truth.

93% of teachers report "high levels of job-related stress"

A recent study conducted by the University of Missouri found that 93 percent of teachers report high levels of stress.[3] I began to wonder what set apart the 7 percent of teachers who did not experience high levels of stress from the masses. It is frightening to know that only 7 percent of teachers feel they have the ability to cope with the demands and stressors of the job.

What exactly makes the job of teaching so stressful? A few things that come to mind include too many classes to prep for and not enough planning time, large class sizes, standardized testing, students "below grade level," attempting to differentiate instruction and meet student needs, and challenging student behaviors. These are just a few of the things that come to mind for me. What might you add to the list? Here are a few additional challenges I've heard from other educators:

- Working hard for five years with no raise.

- Trying to meet the unrealistic expectations set by administrators who have forgotten what it's like to be a teacher.

- Dealing with mental health issues that we are not equipped to handle.

- Realizing that the education system does *not* support all students or teachers.

- Feeling abused by students, helicopter parents, and administrators.

- Working based on policies set by legislators who make the key curriculum and financial decisions without understanding education or how the human brain grows and functions.

- Working in districts that don't meet the basic needs of students or teachers, and the long-term consequences of this issue on students' intelligence and teachers' spirits.

- Evaluations based on how students are performing both in the classroom and on standardized assessments.

- Earning less every year while benefits erode.

- Funding inadequacies for basic supplies and inequitable funding for public versus charter schools.

- Feeling betrayed and very, very angry at how much is stacked against us.

I was concerned for those who were feeling overwhelmed, stressed, and close to burnout prior to the pandemic. Now that we are in the midst of a global pandemic I am even more concerned with how to navigate the demands of the job along with the additional stress of a pandemic and so many other circumstances that are beyond our control.

This pandemic has disrupted the ways in which we connect and conduct our learning and teaching. Many of us left our classrooms without knowing it would be the last time we would occupy that space with our students for the remainder of the school year. We headed home into the unknown with a mixture of emotions and a headful of uncertainty. Grief and confusion became our new companions, and our heads and hearts grew heavy and weary. Around the country, face-to-face learning was suspended, and schools had to quickly adapt and create a system sufficient to respond to our new normal. Creating some sense of order from this chaos and confusion involved pivoting from a system that's been in play for 150 years. We had to figure out how to move forward in a way that prioritized what was most essential so that learning could still occur.

Never before has education experienced such a rapid reinvention in such a short period of time. In addition, we had to develop solutions for other issues that are handled by schools. For example, how do we provide food for our students who rely on the meals they receive from school? How can we make sure that *all* students have access to the internet and technology? How do we engage students in meaningful learning so they continue to thrive regardless of the environment? As educators doing our best to check in with each student, we learned more about each students' home life. Suddenly, we also had to take into account the needs and inequities that are present in our communities. We were left wondering how we would make it through the coming days.

Many of us were already feeling like we were close to our breaking point before this new fear and uncertainty came looming over us. With so much unknown and out of our control, how do we navigate this new norm while carrying all of our grief and sadness, along with our worry and concern? Is it possible to maintain boundaries when our personal and professional lives now occupy the same space? I wonder if this will be the thing that pushes many of today's teachers to consider a new career, resulting in an increase in the number of educators leaving the profession.

A Personal Account of Building Resilience

—Mona S., agricultural education teacher &
Future Farmers of America advisor

COVID-19 invited Dracula into my living room. I became a teacher after working for a few years at an agency that helped those with disabilities live independently. The most rewarding part of the job was teaching kids and young adults skills to help them be successful in life. I wanted more of that kind of work, so I went back to school and trained to be a career and technical education instructor. Now I get to teach and coach high school students to build the skills they will need to be successful adults. These combined roles feed my creativity and fill me with a deep sense of purpose. They can also easily equate to 70-hour work weeks year-round.

After becoming a mom, I realized my work would need to have stricter boundaries around it. Life was busy before, and now I had this amazing little person who needed me to be physically, emotionally, and mentally present, available to meet his needs and build a deep and healthy relationship with him. This realization also showed me that I had been neglecting the same needs in my spouse. This called for a change in my behavior and boundaries around my work.

So, when I was with my family, I started treating work like it was Bram Stoker's Dracula. Stoker's infamous vampire followed many rules, but the rule that helped me the most was the one that mandated that Dracula could only enter a home when invited.

Dracula was invited into our home on occasion, before COVID-19. He was allowed in for grading when my child was sleeping or my spouse was watching sports. Dracula could take me away from home on occasion as coaching and other duties required travel. And, of course, Dracula entered my home whenever my child was sick. But that was it, and I tried to make those exceptions as rare as possible. I learned to limit the amount of time school duties entered my home.

COVID-19 brought Dracula into my house and let him set up a desk in my living room. There he was in the middle of the toys, my family, and my life. When my spouse got sent to work from home as well, his position gave no leeway for the fact that we had a toddler. As a result, I became a full-time mother, playmate, teacher, coach, spouse, cleaning service, and 24-hour kitchen staff.

Dracula wanted me at all hours of the day. I fed Dracula at naptime, after bedtime, on stroller walks, during screen time, during meals, and in the middle of the night. Dracula was everywhere, and the monster slowly drained me of everything I had to give. I found that my school-work was no longer giving me joy. I felt like I couldn't teach effectively, my students were unable to learn effectively, and I was stuck running around worried about how my students were doing, how I wanted to help them, all while recognizing that I couldn't help them. My boundaries were destroyed. When people in my life disrespect my boundaries, we talk about it, reconcile, forgive, and move on. I could not do that with my job, especially not when it was in my living room. My Dracula, like any self-respecting vampire, drained me dry.

My son is a bubbly two-year-old boy. He got locked in his house without warning with his mom, his dad, and our jobs. Before COVID-19, he went to a wonderful daycare where he played and learned with friends. When he came home, he got the full attention of both his parents until bedtime. That all changed with COVID-19. Overnight he was stripped of friends, activities, and our attention.

Life for him after coming home for COVID-19 consisted of mom multitasking through every play time and mealtime. He got to watch a lot more TV and even got his own tablet, but he quickly saw through our attempts to entertain with electronics and found his own entertainment. My son went to war on my work Dracula. Every zoom meeting ended with him pushing the power button on my laptop. Grading? He tore my paperwork to pieces. Answering email on my phone? He would hit, bite, pull hair, or literally pull my glasses off my face and throw them across the room. Dracula got us both.

I was a mess. I ugly cried at least once a day. I disconnected from my work and found it difficult to be present for my kid. I embarrassed myself by losing my cool on more than one occasion. I started having terrible nightmares and what felt like panic attacks in my sleep. My spouse was legitimately concerned that I was losing my mind.

Then one morning my kid expressed his war with Dracula by biting me, pulling my hair, and hitting me with a toy train, all at the same time. And for the first time ever, I felt every parent's worst nightmare. After I had detached him from my body and set him a foot away from me on the couch, he came at me again, and I pushed him. I pushed hard enough that he fell back on the couch. It was not a violent push, or one that could have hurt his body. But we both knew that little shove was a betrayal of the relationship we had built. I knew it in my soul, and I saw it on his face. That was the moment I knew that if I didn't change something, I might hurt the people I love the most because I was hurting too much. I was burned out on my work and on the circumstances of our life during the crisis. Something had to change.

We did the only thing we could do. Because of COVID-19, I could not kick Dracula out of our house. We had to weigh the physical health of our son against my mental health. We made the agonizing decision to reenroll him in daycare. I felt like a failure in both work and motherhood. I knew I would be judged and would contend with mom guilt over this decision for a long time.

As time has gone on, I've learned to frame the decision in the knowledge that we did what was best for our family by doing what was best for me. I come from a long personal and cultural history of feeling guilty about self-care. I was explicitly taught in school, at home, and in church that putting the needs of others above my own was what I was supposed to do. I still feel caring for others is essential to all of our wholeness as people. But if we care for the needs of others, to the detriment of ourselves, what do we become?

I am in recovery from burnout. I am learning how to not feel shame when caring for myself. I wish it was a switch I could just flip, but it isn't. I built a life without much regard for self-care. It's going to take time for me to dismantle and rebuild a new approach that includes self-care. I guess the gift of COVID-19, and of Dracula coming home, is that I caught a glimpse of what my life might be like if I didn't make these necessary changes. A glimpse was enough.

I have plenty of personal work to do, but it's also time to kick Dracula out. As we look at all the uncertainties facing education, my biggest concern is when and how we will regain our right to set boundaries around our work again. Even if we go back to school in some "normal" fashion, the battle changes but does not end. There are plenty of us who had Dracula in our home even before this mess. How do we prepare for and fight the relentless battle we now face? I need help to know how to arm myself against this new Dracula.

I think the biggest step I can take is to remember that I am the boss, not Dracula. We may not be able to kick Dracula out of our homes completely, but we can make him go sit in the yard by himself until we invite him in again. He might be in my house, but I'm still in charge here. I can set hours and adjust my home environment to limit his impact. I can stand up to pressure from kids, parents, or administrators to work at all hours. I can adjust how my students learn our content so it meets my needs as well as theirs. I can adjust how I grade and give feedback so it is manageable and confined to when my son is sleeping or my spouse is watching sports. I can learn and apply more strategies to help me navigate my time at work without it consuming me. I can change my mindset, slow down, and say no. Most importantly, I can tell Dracula and my family when I need a break and I can actually take a break. I can and will be using more leave time in the future. When I'm not on leave I'm going to take time to eat, work out, read, and create outside of school-based activities. The key is to remember there are fixes and to not be ashamed to take steps to fix the problem, regardless of the mom guilt or the teacher guilt I might feel. I am not letting anyone down by taking time to apply a fix to a problem. If they feel let down, that's their issue, their Dracula to deal with.

How Has the Pandemic Impacted You?

The COVID-19 pandemic has impacted us all in one way or another. How has the COVID-19 pandemic impacted you? As you look back over this period of time and reflect on it, can you name what has been *taken away* as a result of it? How about what has remained the same despite the occurrence of it?

Perhaps this sudden disruption that is a result of the COVID-19 pandemic is the perfect time to start reimagining, designing, and building a new way of education. If you were able to reimagine and design a new way of educating, what would it look like?

_____

_____

_____

_____

_____

_____

_____

_____

_____

_____

CHAPTER 4

THE NEW WORLD OF EDUCATION

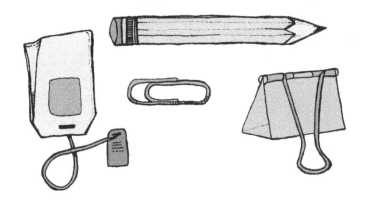

"There are many issues affecting schools today and many changes that need to happen. Nobody knows this more than teachers."

—Sheila Sims, public school teacher

Educators are amazing. They work hard, give tirelessly of themselves, and often help hold communities together. They are often underpaid and underappreciated. In the beginning stages of moving through this pandemic, social media was filled with posts suggesting that educators are amazing for tackling this difficult work on a daily basis and should therefore be paid more money. No disagreement there, but unfortunately it took a pandemic for many outside the field of education to realize the demanding and hard work of educating.

Many educators no longer have the luxury of just focusing on teaching. In addition to teaching the three Rs (reading, writing, and arithmetic), they are now given the task of educating students in all content areas, in addition to meeting behavioral needs and student-specific learning needs. More recently, as academic and behavioral needs of students have continued to change, educators have also started teaching social-emotional learning in ways that develop emotional intelligence and help teach students regulation skills.

The demands don't stop there. As funding continues to decrease and fine arts programs are pulled from schools, educators must get creative in offering these opportunities to students along with the fast-paced shifts in technology. Educators no longer have the luxury of wearing one hat, but many hats and sometimes multiple hats all at once. Educators find themselves functioning as counselors, nurses, friends, parents, advisors, coaches, cheerleaders, mentors, and social workers. The list goes on and on.

If teaching academics was the only thing educators needed to worry about, I am not sure that we would be having this conversation.

Unfortunately, academics are not the only thing educators focus on in a school day. It's not that teachers can't do the job, it's that the job keeps changing and demanding more and more. We have put many educators in situations that seem impossible to maintain, and yet we ask them to do it again and again, year after year.

> "Academics is a minor part of the role I assume as a teacher. I am much more of a mentor or 'parent' to most of my students. My primary job is to help students know they have the ability to do anything they choose and give them the confidence and tools they need to have enough grit to be successful."
> —Mark W., educator

A Personal Account of Building Resilience

—Lisa P., 2nd-grade teacher

You cannot begin to understand what teaching is until you are completely immersed in it. It will be a roller coaster of ugly and beautiful, heartbreaking and heart wrenching, pain and passion, love and hate, anger and joy, and hopeless and hopeful. You will experience the lowest low and the highest high. Our education system is failing so many, and it drastically needs to change. That change will unfortunately take a very long time. New teachers are signing up for a career that is far from fair or perfect, but one that needs the strongest and most passionate people to get us where we need to be. My advice is to draw a *firm* line between work and home. Take time for yourself daily and do all you can to stay healthy, even if it means disappointing people along the way. Connect with coworkers and work together to support each other. Remember, none of you will be any good to your students if you are not taking care of yourself. They need you to be there and present instead of having the perfect lesson plan or cleanest classroom. Each of your students has a story. These stories take time to be revealed and even longer if there is some pain involved. Each child's story needs to be embraced and supported, first, before any learning can occur. That is the real reason why you need to keep showing up.

The Teaching Profession Compared to Others

Is it realistic for us to expect a novice teacher to meet the same demands as an expert teacher? What other profession does this? Do we expect a doctor to be a nurse, receptionist, and insurance agent all at once? How would you support a novice teacher to meet the demands of the job?

_____

_____

_____

_____

_____

_____

_____

_____

_____

_____

_____

_____

CHAPTER 5

TEACHER TURNOVER

"When faced with impossible workloads, endless accountability, a testing culture run riot, and flat or underfunded pay deals year after year, it is all too common for good teachers to leave the profession."

—Mary Bousted, general secretary,
National Education Union[4]

Nearly 30 percent of teachers leave education within the first five years of their careers, and that number increases to 50 percent when considering those who work in high-poverty areas.[5] You read that right, 50 percent! That is a significant number. Losing 50 percent of the teacher population begins to impact the world of education in other capacities as well. Educators are leaving the profession due to feeling underappreciated, overworked, underpaid, and overstressed. With fewer and fewer educators remaining in the profession, and perhaps even expressing their dissatisfaction for the career they initially chose, other individuals become less likely to pursue teaching as a career choice.

Enrollment in educator preparation programs has plummeted by one-third since 2010 and has only continued to fall since then, with some states seeing up to a 50 percent decrease in enrollment.[6] In recent years preservice teaching programs have been more apt to include preparatory experiences, but there is still little to no formal education around the topic of trauma and how to cope with the demands of the job and the effects of high levels of stress, let alone how to begin the process of developing resiliency among educators. This could be a contributing factor to the stress among educators that leads them to being the one marked absent when working with the most diverse populations of students with trauma. Perhaps by nurturing, supporting, and valuing educators, in addition to reducing the stressful workload, the number of individuals leaving the profession could be lowered and education could once again be considered a rewarding career choice.

While providing a professional development opportunity at a local university, I overheard an educator telling preservice teachers, "Don't choose education as your career, even if it's your passion. Don't even consider it until policies and pay improve." When these feelings persist, it is unlikely that educators are going to encourage others to pursue a career in this profession. This then perpetuates the shortage of new educators we are already experiencing. Instead, one would hope that the advice focused on creating a healthy work/life balance and practices of sustainability to do this work, such as:

- "This is a really, really hard job. The benefits and salary don't always make it seem worth it, but if you are dedicated to the work, you will experience an amazing adventure and meet a lot of incredible kids along the way."

- "Be reflective and make note of what you could do differently on your lesson plans, but then consider *and* remember what went well, and what you plan on doing for yourself that day."

- "Know exactly what you are getting into, maintain excellent boundaries to avoid being exploited, and advocate for public education at every opportunity."

A Personal Account of Building Resilience

—Michelle T., kindergarten teacher

The advice I would offer to another individual thinking about becoming a teacher is to consider not going into education. Educators are not paid well, and they are unappreciated on multiple levels and rarely respected by government officials. If someone was adamant about becoming a teacher, I would offer them the following 10 tips:

1. Budget for your classroom (I budget $100 a month and almost always spend it).

2. Communicate wants and needs to your team and administration. Otherwise, keep your complaints to yourself.

3. Get to know your students *and* their parents. The insight will help you teach your students and help them grow as a person.

4. Do *not* take student behavior personally, and consider how to best support each student. There is always a reason for the behavior, it's their way of communicating.

5. Recognize your own biases and work through them or leave them outside of the classroom.

6. Try your best to manage your personal life with the workload—there will *always* be more work to do, so go home, get some rest, and do something for yourself.

7. Join a union and be an advocate for students and educators.

8. Set boundaries!

9. Understand that the job is thankless, but that you are blessed to be trusted with making a positive influence on the lives of children.

10. Spread love and joy; your students won't remember everything, but they will remember how you made them feel.

The impact of teacher turnover doesn't stop there. We know that whenever a teacher leaves a school or the profession, more than likely the meaningful connection with students also becomes disrupted. Students who need consistency the most are often the ones experiencing it the least. In addition, if a school undergoes significant turnover, the overall culture of the school shifts along with it. The practice of maintaining positive relationships over a long period of time has been shown to assist students in gaining more control over their reactions and responses. Relationships with a safe adult are a crucial component for a student's success in school, not only academically but emotionally as well. Unfortunately, when teachers are functioning from a place of feeling overwhelmed, overworked, and neglected, it is likely that students will begin to experience these things as well.

Districts throughout the country are experiencing significant teacher shortages. Some of the potential solutions include cramming kids into classrooms, making the educator-student ratio unsuccessful and out of balance, hiring long-term subs to fill the role of a qualified professional, online learning to fill in the gap, or in the most unfortunate of situations, kids taking charge of their own learning because we can't find an adult to show up. These solutions place an added strain on those who remain, as they step in to offer support. Unfortunately, they then end up becoming overworked as more demands and responsibilities are placed on them. Eventually, the weight of this additional burden moves them closer to feeling burned out.

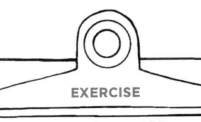

Advice for Potential New Teachers

What advice would you offer someone considering or beginning a career in education?

_____

_____

_____

_____

_____

_____

_____

_____

_____

_____

_____

_____

_____

_____

CHAPTER 6

FOLLOW THE MONEY

Professional development for educators is often a significant financial investment. When an educator leaves, they are leaving on the table the money invested in developing their skill set and expertise. If we believe that this specific knowledge and understanding are beneficial, then we must reinvest that money in another individual or acknowledge that it is no longer an essential skill set.

What would our schools look like if the minimal spending budgets allocated every year were spent on training new employees over and over again to bring them up to speed with their colleagues? According to the Learning Policy Institute, the estimated cost of teacher turnover is $1,155,000. Reducing teacher turnover by 50 percent would save approximately $577,500.[7] An amount of money like that could bring in a whole lot of necessary school supplies and equipment, or be used to offer more support to students and teachers alike.

How long have you been working in education? My guess is that even if it is for only one year, you have given plenty of your personal time and money with the hopes of improving your classroom and instruction for students. Oftentimes teachers take on additional jobs for the sole purpose of being able to afford the items they feel are necessary for the education happening in their classroom. I can't think of many other professions that require you to work an additional job in order to have the materials that help you feel like you are doing your job well.

What would strengthening support do for sustaining new teachers in continuing on in the workplace and reducing teacher turnover? Can you imagine what it would look like to improve the work conditions of all educators? Recent educator strikes and walkouts have now forced communities to take a hard look at how they are negating public education, diminishing the humanity of educators, and creating systems that are underpaid and unsustainable.

We haven't even started talking about increasing compensation for teachers yet. At one point in my career, I was paying a higher hourly rate for childcare than I was making as a tenured teacher. I honestly started questioning why I was teaching and not simply babysitting, and then I remembered the college debt I acquired in order to do the work that I had long dreamed of doing. A mid-career educator's gap in pay can be as wide as 30 percent less compared to that of individuals with college degrees in other fields.[8] We know that most educators don't enter this career because they are motivated by money. However, I don't think that many public school educators anticipated how little their salaries would shift and change over the years. The average salary for a full-time public school educator in the 1999–2000 school year was $59,700. The average salary for educators was $59,000 in the 2011–2012 school year, and increased to a lofty $59,100 in the 2017–2018 school year.[9] These figures are not measurably different even though they span a difference of 18 years. No wonder we have teachers working multiple jobs just to make ends meet. Just imagine what it might be like to be compensated adequately for the work you are doing.

How Would You Spend $500 on Your Classroom?

If you were given an additional $500 to spend on your classroom, how would you use it?

_____

_____

_____

_____

_____

_____

_____

_____

_____

_____

_____

_____

_____

_____

CHAPTER 7

THE WORK-LIFE BALANCING ACT

*"Making it through the school year feels like
a marathon at the pace of a sprint."*

—Koren B., educator

Teaching is beautiful, but it can feel chaotic and overwhelming. When educators become overwhelmed and stretched too thin by the demands of the job, they start to become disengaged. Disengaged teachers are often less effective and eventually, willingly or not, some leave the profession completely.

I held a narrative from my childhood of teachers who gave everything to teach well and make a lasting impact on their community. I now find myself discouraged when I come across similar narratives. I am discouraged because to be lifted up as a good teacher in today's world, it seems as though you must sacrifice everything else in your life.

The popular book *The Freedom Writers Diary* and subsequent film *Freedom Writers* portray an all-too familiar story. A first-year teacher takes a job educating the "tough" kids in an underperforming urban school. Her students are the lowest performing in the school, but she finds a way to help them succeed. However, along the way she sacrifices everything else in her life. She gives up all of her free time, her marriage, and at times, her reputation. After being with these students for four years, she eventually leaves her job in public education. This narrative supports the statistics that educators often leave the profession within the first five years, especially if working with "high poverty/ low performing" populations.

When we do remain in the profession, over time we may start to ask how we can have a greater impact beyond the walls of our classroom. We long to do more with our expertise and our desire to help kids. This may lead us through the natural progression of moving up the education chain from a classroom educator to a team leader teacher and then an administrator. Regardless of what position we fill, with each change, the expectations, along with our responsibilities, begin to change and grow. During this time, we are also growing in our personal lives. We may find a partner we long to share our days with or purchase a new home. We may begin to build our family by adding little people into the mix. Previously "free" evenings and weekends become filled with toys, bath time, and bedtime cuddles and chats. Soon the days are filled with not only the demands of our job, but with the demands of our daily realities.

But then a tension begins to set in.

> "The challenge of feeling like I didn't do enough is the thing that keeps me up at night."
> —Sonja S., educator

We start our careers in education because we want to make a difference and have an impact. We certainly don't do this work for the money. But we have things that we long to accomplish and do within our personal life. Along the way, we may impose unrealistic expectations on ourselves and may feel as though we can never say no to the things that have to do with our career for fear of being perceived as lazy or ungrateful for opportunities. We work our tails off and do anything to earn that "gold star," even if it means putting everyone else's needs, wants, and desires ahead of our own. We keep sacrificing our body, mind, and spirit.

Sometimes the tension builds and grows, causing us to say no to certain things, oftentimes within our personal lives. This pushes us to a place of greater tension and, eventually, we may come to learn that saying no is acceptable, or our body and mind say no for us, leading some to reach the conclusion that the only solution is to leave our current position in order to sustain. No matter how hard we work, we may assume it is not enough. Leaving our work may bring about feelings of inadequacy as we fall short of our expectations, even when they were perhaps impossible. Still, feelings of criticism, guilt, and shame begin to set in, leaving us feeling exhausted.

Seeking Balance

Do you feel like it is possible to obtain a sense of work-life balance? What emotions accompany these thoughts?

_____

_____

_____

_____

_____

_____

_____

_____

_____

_____

_____

_____

_____

_____

_____

CHAPTER 8

MINIMIZING THE DEMANDS ON OUR TIME

In our attempts to balance it all, we often become overwhelmed. We then begin to feel immobilized by having to make even the simplest of decisions. This decision-making fatigue is why we struggle to choose what to make for dinner at the end of the day, or whether or not to go to the gym. When these feelings persist and the to-do list becomes a mile long, it becomes even more important for us to consider how to make the significant step to prioritize our own well-being.

In *The Minimalist Home,* Joshua Becker defines minimalism as "the intentional promotion of things we most value and the removal of anything that distracts us from them."[10] I started to think about this not only in connection to my personal life, but in connection to educators and how it impacts their work and personal life. Then I started considering if minimizing isn't somehow like optimizing.

The good news is that we can minimize, or lighten the load, of our daily decision-making and tasks. Through planning, time management, and boundary setting, we can set limits and maximize our time to promote more of the things we value most. Before Monday morning rolls around again, we can put some things into place to support our overall well-being. For example, we can take time for meal planning and prep in order to promote healthy eating, set times to check our work email on the job rather than at home, establish a routine to support health and wellness, and design a schedule that includes time to support ourselves each day upon leaving work. These are just a few examples of how we can reduce the daily decision-making and minimize the things that demand our attention.

A Personal Account of Building Resilience

—Marjoree D., public school teacher

When I reflect on my years of service in the classroom, the most valuable advice I can provide is a cautionary tale about boundaries, exceptions, and limits. By sharing my personal experience, I hope I can bring a sense of compassion to other educators who may have struggled under similar circumstances. I'm also hopeful that some can better understand the duality that many educators face. The conflict comes from having deep, powerful, and bottomless passion about being a teacher. But attempting to accurately match the amount of work you do to the intensity of passion that you have will leave you utterly exhausted. Especially when your effectiveness and value as an employee is measured by the amount of successful work completed, instead of the intensity of your passion and the purity of your intentions.

It took me years to learn how to feel successful. I kept waiting for my hard work to be enough and for the late nights and sacrifices in my personal life to deliver me into a space where I could feel proud, valued, and confident. And, I wanted to do it while still feeling whole. It took me years to learn how to give myself permission to say no and trust that it was okay to say it.

My first teaching position was unique in that I taught in a single district building/charter school. The school was staffed with some of the most caring and ambitious people I've ever met (sometimes too ambitious). Together we collaborated closely to try and implement innovative, nontraditional teaching practices that we believed in.

All of us accepted several additional tasks and responsibilities outside of our job descriptions and instructional duties. We knew that it was crucial for us to fill the gaps that could have been filled if we had the resources of a larger, more financially robust school district. Despite the extraordinary demands, we pushed forward with our vision. Many educators burned out and began to leave their positions. These were brilliant and talented educators. Some even left the profession altogether because of their experiences there. This led to additional increases in the workloads of those who decided to stay and tough it out. Inevitably, this created a toxic staff culture that offered more harm than good. What would have been considered an overachievement at a typical school was considered "a good start" there.

We wanted so badly for our students to succeed and we wanted to prove that the model of instruction that we were developing was measurably effective. But if the to-do list never ends, when do we have time to feel like successful educators?

How can we feel proud and celebrate the work we've completed, when all of the pressure and attention is placed on what wasn't done on time, or what wasn't "detailed" or "thorough" enough? Constructive criticism has its place in the academic world, but I'm not sure if constant criticism does. What we needed was positive affirmation, support, flexibility, and recognition from our administrators for the astounding amount of effort, time, and action that we were cultivating from within ourselves to try and meet these impossible expectations.

I began documenting the number of hours I was working in addition to my contract hours, and I had a total of 80 hours on the busiest weeks. My time spent in meetings totaled eight hours by the end of some weeks. My inner dialogue shifted to lectures about how I couldn't survive the pressures of a teaching career. My inner self was telling me to escape, quit, or somehow find a way out because failure felt imminent. I felt I had no other choice but to leave, or confront my administrators to try to explain the effect that these expectations were having on my mental health.

I told them how the hours added up. I skipped the part about being so stressed I could not sleep at night.

I told them about my need to feel successful and tried my best to connect this to how we might accommodate the different learning needs of my students.

I skipped the part about my recurring panic attacks, or having to pull my car over on my way into work because the worry and stress of the day ahead often made me physically ill.

I told them that I needed something to change.

I tried my best to let them know this wasn't a whine or a petty request for easier work. I had to trust that being vulnerable and transparent about my mental health challenges could help change my work conditions and even offer some insight into how other teachers there were feeling.

Their response? They listened. They saw me as a human being with good intentions and natural flaws. We shared a dialogue with one another, which allowed me to express how and when I was experiencing increased anxiety and feeling "triggered" during my routines. These meetings also gave me a platform to bring trauma into the conversation. This profession requires learning and introspection from everyone involved: students, parents, teachers, administrators, everyone.

So my advice, don't wait until you're against a wall to push back. Saying no isn't a reflection of your work ethic, attitude, or abilities. It is a way to communicate personal boundaries and ask for support. I wish I had learned this earlier on in my career. I learned firsthand and from watching others the importance of self-care and resilience. I have time now where I had none before because of routines and decisions I made and prioritized, and now I see a rewarding and prolific future as an educator.

The problem was fixed not because I left or complained to my coworkers, and not because of a raise, award, or a new program. The problem was fixed because I made a decision to be resilient.

Ways to Lighten Your Load

What decisions can you make before Monday morning that would lighten your load and reduce some of the anxiety you might feel on a Sunday evening or as you move throughout the week? Are there routines that can become a part of how you start or end each day that allow for reflection and rest? How can you maximize your sense of wholeness (instead of sacrificing it) by prioritizing and using your time differently?

_____

_____

_____

_____

_____

_____

_____

_____

_____

_____

_____

_____

CHAPTER 9

HOW EFFECTIVE IS HIGHLY EFFECTIVE?

In James H. Stronge's book, *Qualities of Effective Teachers*, he states that "Effectiveness is an elusive concept when we consider the complex task of teaching. Some researchers define teacher effectiveness in terms of student achievement. Others focus on high performance ratings from supervisors. Still others rely on comments from students, administrators, and other interested stakeholders."[11] Regardless of what you focus on to determine the effectiveness of an educator, an effective teacher should be effective for all.

The term "highly effective" can elicit strong emotions depending on the weight it carries for an individual. How many days did it take parents to start feeling ineffective and insufficient at educating their children during those early months of the pandemic? I've sat across from numerous colleagues as they grappled with their effectiveness, questioning themselves and wondering if they are doing a good enough job or are even meant to do this work. Over the years they may fluctuate back and forth between effective and highly effective ratings, when all that is really changing is the students who are present in the room. I once had an evaluation by both a principal and department supervisor. Though they observed and experienced many of the same things regarding my teaching and instruction, they rated my effectiveness quite differently. So, perhaps, it does indeed depend on who is walking into the room.

Many educators hold onto the perception that if they can't do it all and if they begin to feel overwhelmed on a daily basis, then they must be doing something wrong. There is this internalized perception that they are the result of their struggle. If they could just do better, then the workload would be easier to bear. They could then become a highly effective teacher. What system is at play when these thoughts come to mind?

But I wonder, who is an effective teacher and how is it defined? Determining who is or isn't a highly effective educator can be difficult to do. Our strengths show up in different aspects of teaching based on our personalities, our passion, and our experience. It is unrealistic to expect that highly effective educators would excel at doing it all, and yet we have a hard time accepting fragmented excellence. This drives us to believe the misconception that in order to be a highly effective educator, one must show up early, stay late, and give up even more of their free time on weekends. In addition, it may become necessary to deny their individual needs or the needs of their family, and possibly become someone who sacrifices movement, nourishment, and rest. Is that what makes someone a highly effective teacher? Does being an educator need to become your sole identity in order to be considered a highly effective teacher?

Teacher evaluations have shifted significantly over the past 10 years to include ratings from unsatisfactory to highly effective. These ratings are given in reference to a variety of domains, similar to those outlined in the Danielson Framework: Planning and Preparation, Classroom Environment, Instruction, and Professional Responsibilities.[12] Each domain consists of multiple subcategories and things to look for to determine the effectiveness of an educator and their teaching.

Now think about your students. As a caring educator, would you expect your students to walk into your classroom already knowing and excelling at everything, regardless of the circumstances they encountered prior to entering your classroom? The answer is no because you know that that mindset does not acknowledge our humanness or promote growth. Instead, we work to determine where a student is at and then give them digestible and incremental steps, moving them through the zones of proximal development (ZPD) so they can go from completing a task with guidance to completing it independently. Yet, despite knowing the effectiveness of working within a student's ZPD, we fail to offer ourselves the same supportive and caring approach. We have a tendency to hold ourselves to a higher, unrealistic standard to measure our effectiveness and success within our work.

Interestingly enough, Stephen Covey, who wrote the best-selling book *The Seven Habits of Highly Effective People,*[13] shares how taking care of yourself is one of the seven habits that is an essential part to achieving success. It is unfortunate that a component of our yearly educator evaluation and our conversations with administrators do not include the use of the effective habit of taking care of oneself, since its application ultimately impacts how we educate and care for our students in the long run.

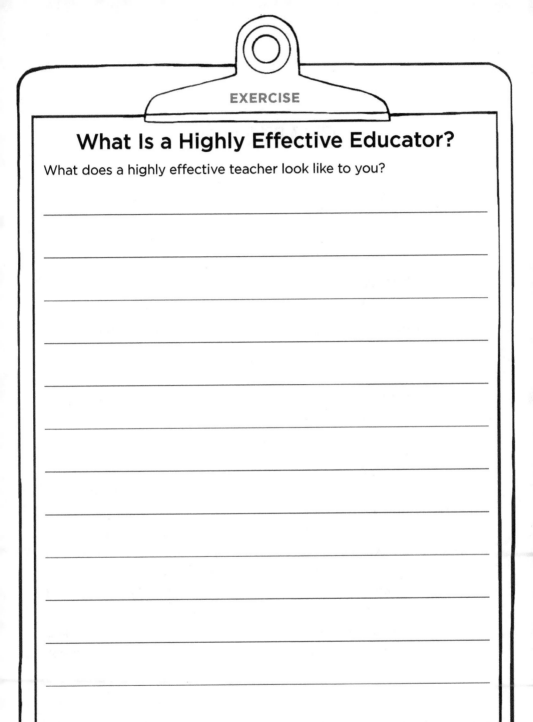

What Is a Highly Effective Educator?

What does a highly effective teacher look like to you?

CHAPTER 10

WHAT GETS NOTICED

"Teachers rarely, if ever, get to have quiet time or bad days. We have to keep pushing on despite any personal discomfort we might be feeling."

—Sasha G., educator

"Teacher of the Year" awards are a notable honor to obtain. However, I often wonder what it is that we are honoring and celebrating when handing out these awards.

I once listened to a colleague express her disappointment that the "Teacher of the Year" award went to a colleague who was teaching full time, acting as the interim assistant principal when necessary, coaching basketball, and served on multiple school committees. The disappointment was not directed toward the individual who had won the award, but toward herself and the acknowledgment that she had her limits. She was an individual who was also teaching full time and participated in several school committees. However, she was also raising two children and made the decision to leave work every evening at six o'clock to take her children home, prepare a home-cooked meal, and spend some time together before tucking them into bed.

Another teacher confided to me that her celebrated and successful career as an educator came with a severe cost. Her success took a toll on her seven-year marriage, which ended in divorce. It meant that her children spent more waking hours being parented by someone other than herself. In fact, she often had to send a relative to attend her children's school functions because she could not take the time away from work. As the tears fell from her eyes, she acknowledged that the cost of her success in her career came at the cost of her family.

I worry about the mob mentality that can take over in education and cause us to lose our sense of self. Mob mentality, as defined by Wikipedia,[14] is "how people can be influenced by their peers to adopt certain behaviors." Ever feel pressured, intentionally or not, to show up in a certain way? When people are influenced by mob mentality, they begin to make decisions rooted in emotions. In addition, they may feel the need to conform to the habits, behaviors, and ways of thinking exhibited by their colleagues, rather than make decisions that are best for them as individuals. There may even be a sense of polarization among staff when perceptions of those who care and those who don't are pinned against each other.

I don't think anyone intentionally signs up to go with the flow and join the masses, particularly when it aligns with unhealthy and harmful behaviors toward ourself or others. Unfortunately, it's easy to get overwhelmed and overridden even when it is harming ourselves or others. It certainly takes a lot of courage to pull back from the "mob" and evaluate what is best for you as an individual, and then be confident in how you choose to move forward, especially if this looks different from the masses.

CAN THE WORK GET DONE IN A DIFFERENT KIND OF WAY?

New Ways to Approach Your Work

If you were to approach your work in a different kind of way, what would it look like?

_____

_____

_____

_____

_____

_____

_____

_____

_____

_____

_____

_____

CHAPTER 11

THE MYTH OF "BUSYNESS"

*"Don't confuse being busy with being productive.
Just because you're busy all the time doesn't
mean you're getting closer to your goals."*

—Karen McKenna, MusicThoughts contributor

"Productive" and "busy" should not be held as synonyms. Busyness and productivity can play out in our daily lives in significantly different ways. The common phrase "work smarter, not harder" encourages us to consider the ways in which we are working.

In *The Creative Classroom* podcast episode "The Difference Between Being Busy and Being Productive," John Spencer "breaks up with busy" to become more productive, after recognizing the impact his busyness was having on the people he cared the most about. He says, "You don't get a trophy for packing your schedule with more projects and more accomplishments and more meetings. All you get is a bigger load of busy. But busy is hurried. Busy is overwhelmed. Busy is fast."

Some of the characteristics of busyness include responding quickly, attempting to fit in too many things, driving for perfection, multitasking, and being distracted by urgency.

"Productivity is never an accident. It is always the result of a commitment to excellence, intelligent planning, and focused effort."

—Paul J. Meyer, author of *Unlocking Your Legacy: 25 Keys for Success*

On the other hand, characteristics of productivity include creating goals and prioritizing, having purpose, taking a "less is more" approach, focusing, and knowing when to take a break.

When we experience an increase in our workload or in stress, we may notice that our attention, ability to concentrate, and perhaps even our productivity decreases for the time being. The extent of the impact from this stress is determined by how easily we can shift and reprioritize, and break the cycle of busyness.

In a profession that values performance, we must remember that our value *does not* increase when we decrease the time we take to care for ourselves. How many meals, bathroom breaks, and moments with friends and family have you skipped to grade papers, write lesson plans, and meet deadlines placed by others? These shortcuts do not promote our well-being. Instead they create bad habits that promote busyness and put others in front of our own basic needs. Teachers should not have to take a leave of absence or leave the profession in order to get back to meeting basic human needs. While it is admirable to try and meet the needs of all people or accomplish every task, we risk experiencing burnout when we try to be good at all things, all the time.

It can be difficult to shift our mentality, especially when those around us might not be moving in similar ways. Angela Watson, founder of the 40 Hour Teacher Workweek,[15] recognizes the importance of shifting from busy to productive within the world of education. As a national board-certified teacher and instructional coach, she understands the demands of education and helps guide educators through the process of organizing and optimizing their time with more purpose. Rather than add more hours to the day, she shows educators how to make the hours in the day more meaningful and productive. I am grateful that this program exists, but I wonder, "What if this practice was supported by our administrators and colleagues?"

> "Be sure to find ways to balance your time and take care of yourself. There is always more to do, but your time is limited."
> —Micah H., educator

Busy should not be a badge of honor. Our value should not be determined by how many hours we stay at school, how many committees we are on, or how many people depend on us.

A Personal Account of Building Resilience

—Terese W., 1st-grade teacher

I am a proud product of Detroit public schools. After graduating with a degree in secondary education, I immediately returned to Detroit to teach high school English. The years I spent teaching there were some of the most rewarding of my career—I loved my work and planned to do it for years. However, after only a few years teaching there, I moved with my spouse to the other side of the state and began teaching in a public district that was more racially, socioeconomically, and politically diverse. It was here that I was confronted with what is often termed the "achievement gap" as measured by the tools of a K-12 system shaped by racism and white supremacy—grades, test scores, "disciplinary" referrals, and more. I was equally angry and motivated by the disparities. Why do they happen? When do they happen? What do they mean? How do we stop them? In an effort to really investigate these questions, I went back to school to earn both my elementary and early childhood endorsements. It was then, in my work with young children, that I began to understand the complexity of educational inequity that begins before birth.

When we really begin to realize how racism, white supremacy, and patriarchy are so deeply ingrained in educational systems, it makes sense that hopelessness and burnout follow. Nearly every day, I recognize injustice in my district, school, and classroom. Our test scores, suspensions, "discipline" statistics, and more are racialized and gendered. Our teaching force does not remotely represent the students we serve. Many of our policies are built upon white supremacist ideals and then inequitably enforced. Our curricula do not teach the hard truths accurately or fully, let alone recognize the contributions, joy, and resilience of black and brown people.

Whether I like to admit it or not, the most discouraging moments are those in which I recognize my own complicity in oppression. For example, when I fail to effectively advocate for a student subjected to a "zero tolerance" policy. When I perpetuate the inequitable policing of bodies and white expectations of behavior through "school norms and expectations." When I "cave under pressure" and "teach to the test," even when I know it is not the best way to teach or learn. I could go on and on. These are the moments and issues that wear me down, break my heart, and bring me even closer to burnout. Yet, simultaneously, these are also the moments and issues that motivate me to keep going. I know that it is my responsibility to do better, to resist, and to continue to learn to be an anti-racist, abolitionist educator.

While I do not hesitate to take on challenges, I know that, unless I do it in manageable chunks, I get overwhelmed and the challenges seem insurmountable. I need to set achievable goals and priorities. I need focus. I know that to be a highly effective educator I must continue to learn to be an anti-racist, abolitionist one. In order for me to be a healthy teacher and human, while owning this imperative to live in a way that furthers justice, I seek out learning through a logical, recursive process of focus and priority setting. This is what it looks like in my life:

1. Rejuvenate and Reflect

This work begins for me each summer. I feel rejuvenated by the family time, the sun, the warmth, and my frequent visits to Lake Michigan (my happy place). I feel deeply grateful for one of the great graces of teaching—each year, you get to try again. So, I reflect on my successes and failures of the previous year. What is it that I want to do better? To understand more deeply? To apply to my future teaching?

2. Focus and Prioritize

There is so much to learn. There are so many brilliant people who have created and shared so much. It is all important. There is no way I can learn it all. So, I choose a focus. This summer, for example, in the midst of a global pandemic and a surge in racial justice uprisings and awareness across the country, I poured my time and energy into learning about "abolitionist teaching" and social emotional learning in service of racial justice. This has become my priority.

3. Immerse

I throw myself fully and completely into learning all I can about the topic. I email everyone I know with expertise and ask questions. What books should I check out? Who should I follow? I read and read and read and read. I research. I listen to podcasts. I watch webinars. I take notes in a notebook dedicated to this topic. I talk to my friends and spouse about it. I get to know the names of the most respected scholars and practitioners. I find and attend professional developments either online or in the area. I reach out in every way I can to immerse myself in learning all I can.

4. Seek Community

I seek out relationships with like-minded people and coworkers who further my understanding, challenge my thinking, and inspire me. I join social media networks on Twitter or Facebook. Even better are the professional groups and organizations I can join in person. I was recently invited to join a county-wide group of educators and administrators in pursuit of learning to teach math in an anti-racist, culturally-relevant, brain-based way to diminish and hopefully abolish racialized outcomes. That group has been essential in my well-being. It is a safe space in which I feel supported and accepted, while also challenged and pushed outside of my comfort zone. I leave those meetings—even when they follow exhausting full days of school—feeling inspired and ready to go back to work the next day with a renewed commitment.

5. Apply

With my rested body, my new learning, my renewed commitment, and my relationships and communities alongside me, I feel ready to enter my classroom with a new perspective. I simply cannot think about every single variable as I design each lesson, make each decision, have each conversation. But I can set my priorities and filter everything through this lens. For example, with my current focus on anti-racist and abolitionist teaching, I ask myself multiple times a day: Does my response to this behavior reflect and model respect for all children? Does this policy perpetuate or resist white supremacist norms? How can this lesson acknowledge and build upon the brilliance and joy of my students, especially my students of color?

I think it's important to acknowledge that, even when I employ this process with fidelity, I fall short constantly and have days, weeks, or even months where I do not feel resilient. Particularly in the "application" phase, when I bring all my passion and excitement and new learning into my school and classroom, I am met with resistance, shut down, discouraged, and frankly exhausted by the constant battle. That's when I go back to the community, the people, and the relationships. I lean on other teachers, supportive parents, and my beloved students. I re-watch the webinars. I go back to the quotes underlined in the books I've read. I go to meetings with other educators. I cry...a lot.

Teaching is hard work. There are so many constraints, and so much is out of our control. But teachers are powerful. We have discretion and agency. And there are so many people out there giving us opportunities to learn to be better and stronger and more creative and more revolutionary. I am a healthier teacher and person when I acknowledge all that we are up against, look outside of myself for help and community, and then make a choice to refine my focus and establish priorities. Over and over again. What can I do today that will bring about justice? What can I do tomorrow? Definitely not everything. But absolutely something. I constantly reevaluate what that something is, learn more and get better at it, practice it every day until it becomes normal, and then when I am ready, add something else.

How Can You Maximize the Use of Your Time?

What can you do to reduce the "busyness" in your life and maximize the use of your time?

_____

_____

_____

_____

_____

_____

_____

_____

_____

_____

_____

CHAPTER 12

A NEW DEFINITION OF A HIGHLY EFFECTIVE EDUCATOR

"I set boundaries with my time. I work daily on self-awareness. I am very careful to protect my health and wellness. I have a large network of support. I try to accept the things I cannot control. I make an intentional choice to keep my stress levels lower by only teaching 50 percent of the time and job sharing, so I am not giving my all to my job and not having what I need to be highly effective in other areas of my life."

—Martha R., educator

Does a highly effective educator have to give an endless amount of their time and attention to work in order to meet all expectations? Or, can an outstanding educator be someone who values *not* being all things to all people but instead, an individual who focuses on specific goals and priorities?

Let's explore what a "highly effective" educator could look like and how the reimagined version could offer benefits to that individual as well as to their students, families, and the world of educators as a whole. I believe that these reimagined "highly effective educators" can:

- Be a human *and* an educator
- Stop feeling guilty
- Set goals for *both* inside and outside of their career
- Promote and practice a healthy work-life balance
- Find time to care for themselves *and* others
- Practice boundaries
- Feel okay saying no
- Give their colleagues permission to say no as well
- Take a mental health day
- Ask for help
- Be confident in their decisions

I believe we can be *both* an educator and a human. Even better, I believe we can do our best and not be ashamed about the work we do, or even more importantly, the work we don't do. We still need to work hard but accept that we might not get it all done. We need to learn to set work boundaries, tell ourselves it is okay to go home, and not feel ashamed when we do.

Remember that you are a human first and an educator second.

Let's cheer each other on and honor our humanness and the roles we fill outside of our career in education. Let's declare with boldness that "it's okay to be done for today." Let's lift each other up and use our voices to bring reminders of truth, encouragement, and balance, and give others permission to do the same. Let's silence the voice that whispers "you are not enough."

What Does a Reimagined Effective Educator Look Like to You?

What would a reimagined "highly effective educator" look like to you? Is a 40-hour work week a reality for educators and, if so, what would this mean for them, their students, their families, and education as a whole?

_____

_____

_____

_____

_____

_____

_____

_____

_____

_____

_____

_____

_____

PART II

The Ripple Effect of Trauma

CHAPTER 13

TEACHING THROUGH RISK

Prior to this historic and life-altering pandemic, educators walked into schools on a daily basis knowing that they were taking a calculated risk by being there. In large part, the biggest risk factor used to be the unimaginable occurrence of a school shooting. Regardless of the protective measures and training put into place, there could never be a 100 percent guarantee that our lives would not be at risk should this occur. Even though we are told we don't have to be the last one out of the room, it seems unimaginable to hold the lives of children below our own.

Then COVID-19 showed up, disrupting life as we know it.

Children were suddenly ripped out of their routines and normalcy. Families were thrown into consistent close proximity and suddenly had to figure out how to navigate living, working, and learning coherently, along with a mound of other unknowns. And educators had to make a quick pivot and work through all of this and more to offer some sense of normalcy to families and students. Distance learning and working was an adjustment for many of us, especially those who had to simultaneously parent while working from home. Distance learning is no substitute for the teaching and learning that happens when we are together in person. But somehow, we made it through those first few months of living with COVID-19, finally making it to the end of a crazy and unpredictable school year.

When we shifted into the summer months, the time when most teachers try to recover from the demands of the previous year, educators continued to live in a period of uncertainty. We anxiously awaited to hear what the "new normal" created by COVID-19 would look like.

No teacher became an educator to work remotely and virtually from home. Many of us are eager to get back into close proximity with our students, colleagues, and community. We also know that many students rely on the support services that schools provide to fill in the gaps. We care for the safety of our students and their families, but that doesn't mean that we aren't nervous about our own safety and well-being.

As communities and districts decide how to move forward, will they choose what's best for the well-being of the children, their families, or the teachers? What if these don't all require the same action to move forward? Whose well-being gets priority? The in-between world of what is and what is to come can be a scary place. And dealing with change in general isn't easy or comfortable.

Teachers are paid with taxpayers' money. We serve the children and families of our communities. But who is serving educators and considering our well-being? Are teachers considered expendable and easily replaceable?

In a job that often pays so little, educators with prior health concerns are in an even more precarious position during this pandemic. Do they teach from classrooms during the pandemic and potentially put their life at more risk, or do they leave their career permanently, even before intending to do so? What happens when a student tests positive for COVID-19 and educators are asked to quarantine for 14 days? Does the time off count against their sick leave? If so, what happens if later that educator becomes sick or needs to care for a family member who falls ill? Do they then have to take a dock in pay? In communities with a substitute teacher shortage, how do we ensure we will have enough teachers to provide coverage for those out sick or in quarantine? If there is a substitute teacher shortage, how realistic is it to ask teachers to give even more of themselves by stepping in to fill in the gaps? Are we asking teachers to decide between life and livelihood?

It seems as if the biggest risk now isn't school shootings, but COVID-19 and our responses to a pandemic. How do we communicate our care, concern, and value to those around us? There will be disagreements and anxiety surrounding the decisions made as we move forward. These moments of disagreement and anxiety will require even more of our courage and bravery.

One might think that the biggest risk associated with being an educator is school shootings or the COVID-19 pandemic, but it is actually something that occurs much more frequently. Perhaps this will come as no surprise to you, but the biggest threat to an educator's well-being is stress. Are you surprised?

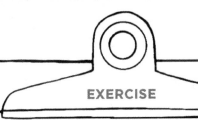

The Risks of Teaching

How were you prepared for the potential risks you would experience in your career? What are some risks you have experienced in your career as an educator? How do these risks impact you mentally, emotionally, and physically?

_____

_____

_____

_____

_____

_____

_____

_____

_____

_____

_____

_____

_____

_____

_____

CHAPTER 14

THE EFFECT OF STRESS

Stress is something we all experience, but it differs from person to person. We each experience variance in the stressors that knock us off balance. How we navigate stress is impacted by the way in which we view our stress, the degree of stress, the way in which we carry that stress, and how it shows up within our bodies. Some of our predisposition to stress is based on genetics and the environment, so to a degree it remains somewhat out of our control. As we grow older and our responsibilities increase, our stress load most likely increases as well.

In moments of stress, our body produces more adrenaline and cortisol. Cortisol, the primary stress hormone, acts like an alarm system to warn us when we encounter danger. The adrenaline increases our energy, heart rate, and even our blood pressure. When experiencing stress, we may have additional physical symptoms such as irritability, headaches, upset stomach, difficulty concentrating or sleeping, and fatigue.[16]

Some forms of stress, at times, can be helpful. This is the "good" part of stress. It activates our adrenaline and cortisol and gets us moving to take action, try harder, and meet deadlines. It's often thought of as what helped us survive the early days of caveman living. However, stress is primarily meant to help us deal with short-term problems, not frequent or ongoing long-term ones.

One of the biggest threats to our well-being is physical and emotional stress. While not necessarily a life-and-death situation, when we encounter stressful situations such as an unpleasant phone call from a parent or a disruptive student, or when we must meet deadlines or perform evaluations, our nervous system responds to these stressful events with the same sense of urgency.[17] As our stress load increases, our energy is depleted and we may feel as though things become unmanageable even more quickly.

There are a variety of ways to lighten your stress load. Things like asking for a hug, engaging in a breathing exercise, getting outside, listening to music, singing or dancing, or having a moment of quiet (we rarely sit in silence, so intentionally seeking it out can help you feel calmer).

The Community Resiliency Model, created by Elaine Miller-Karas, offers the following activities as a way to get "help now" and move back into a "resilient zone" so you find yourself in a grounded state:[18]

1. Walk.

2. Push against a wall.

3. Look for colors and shapes.

4. Count backwards.

5. Drink a beverage.

6. Touch objects.

7. Notice the temperature.

8. Listen for sounds.

9. Notice everything around you.

10. Open your eyes.

The Biggest Threat to an Educator's Well-Being

What percentage of your day do you experience in a state of stress? What are some of the things that add to your daily stress level, and how does this impact other areas of your life? Are the ways you typically deal with your stress helpful? How do you care for your physical, mental, and emotional health to combat these stressors?

CHAPTER 15

THE POTENTIAL FOR CHRONIC STRESS

Most days in the life of an educator are extremely intense. As more and more parents become responsible for their children's learning during the pandemic, COVID-19 is providing some insight into this reality. The structure of a school day is rigid, fast-paced, and filled with overwhelming experiences. Every minute is planned out. Teachers are often on decision-making overload, leaving them fatigued by the end of the day. In addition, students are often unpredictable, bringing into the classroom all of their experiences from their home and personal lives. As students advance in grade levels, challenges from the use of technology and social media also come into play. Teachers are expected to teach a classroom of 30-plus students and manage any and all behavioral problems that present themselves. If you are lucky, you work in a school with multiple paraprofessionals, interventionists, and perhaps even a school counselor and social worker. Sadly, many of us work in schools where little to no additional support is offered.

It is a lot to navigate, especially when you feel like you are doing the best you can under very challenging circumstances. So, perhaps, despite your best efforts, you fall short and occasionally fail to meet all the needs of your students or complete all of the numerous tasks you've been assigned. At the end of that long work day, full of so much, you go home feeling like a failure. When this is the feeling you experience day after day, the work begins to wear you down.

"Prolonged stress may increase risk of chronic fatigue, heart disease, and other ailments. Stress also depletes mental stamina. Common symptoms include irritability, mood swings, and exhaustion, which may escalate into depression, anxiety, and a lower quality of life. These symptoms have been identified by teachers reporting high stress. The consequences, however, do not stop with teachers."[19]

—Brandis M. Ansley, Joel Meyers, et al., authors of "The Hidden Threat of Teacher Stress"

Over a long period of time, the impact of continual stress begins to change. Our bodies are unable to recover and return to a "normal" state because we constantly feel as though we are under attack. The ongoing activation of the stress response means that the body is continually exposed to adrenaline and cortisol, which is helpful in small doses but becomes harmful during constant exposure. This constant, consistent exposure is considered chronic stress. Chronic stress puts your health at risk and is associated with a range of problems, including occupational burnout.[20] Some of the additional health risks include heart disease, anxiety and depression, weight gain, loss of memory and concentration, and sleep problems, to name a few.[21] We may feel confusion as we attempt to reconcile how the work we have long dreamed of doing is now causing us pain and sadness.

Educators can quickly succumb to chronic stress if we aren't careful. That is why it is essential to understand the role of stress and identify healthy ways to cope with it throughout our lifetime.

A Personal Account of Building Resilience

—Jeff V., middle school science teacher

I wasn't a new teacher. I had been teaching for 10 years, but I had a complete breakdown as a teacher. I had taken a new job, sort of a dream job. It was for a small and very progressive inner-city school. The kind of school that saw education differently, or so I thought.

I knew three weeks before school started that I was in trouble. I could not stop the voices in my head that told me something wasn't right. I started having trouble sleeping, and for the first time in my life, I was dealing with crippling anxiety. Almost immediately, I felt it everywhere—my relationships were off, and things that used to bring me joy were empty. Everywhere I went, people asked me about the new job. I would fake a smile and tell myself once school started and I got to build relationships with my 2nd graders, everything would be okay.

It wasn't. I really did love my kids, but everything else was falling apart. The reasons I was falling apart at this new school were many, but for this story, they aren't important. I came home from the first day of school and knew I wasn't going to make it the year. After day seven, a coworker smiled at me and made a comment about surviving another day, "only 173" more was my response. She looked at me like it was a joke, but I knew how many days were left and had counted every single one.

I was in trouble. My wife knew it, my kids knew it, my parents knew it, and I think some coworkers knew it. Any other job in the world, the solution would have been simple: walk away. But teaching isn't any job, it is a calling, it is a responsibility. There is no way I could walk away from these 2nd graders. So, I continued counting my days, trying to invest in the kids and slowly dying inside.

About four weeks, in I had a doctor's appointment. My blood pressure was way higher than it had ever been and my doctor put me on a blood pressure medicine. It was in the doctor's office I had my first real conversation about walking away. It terrified me. I was not a quitter. I had a young student who had been in foster care his whole life, and for the first time in his life, he was making progress. He trusted me. I had another student who was being bullied, and I was his pro-tector. I had another student who was homeless and we had built a great relationship. I couldn't walk away from these kids—they did not deserve it. None of this was their fault.

I think sometimes we, as teachers, view ourselves as saviors, but what I was finding out was that I was on my way to becoming a martyr. My wife began to beg me to walk away. My dad did the same. So, after 37 days, I scheduled a meeting with my principal and made the tough-est decision of my life. I was choosing my family. I was choosing my health, but I was letting so many people down. The next few weeks were not fun. There were hard conversations, disappointed kids, and mad coworkers. There were sleepless nights and many tears. I ended it as well as I possibly could. I blessed each of my kids and then walked away. It was hard and scary. And the scariest part to me was this one thought, "What if I regretted this decision for the rest of my life?"

This is what I want you to take away from my story: I have never once regretted walking away. I miss those kids, I mourned for what I had hoped would be a dream job but never once have I second-guessed my decision. Sometimes you need to save yourself, and that is what I did. I didn't heal as soon as I walked away; that took time and some work, but I did heal.

As I write this, I am about to start a new school year. I am teaching at another school and have spent the last few weeks planning. My wife has made many comments about how she sees joy in me again, and I feel it. I am laughing more and finding joy everywhere. I am myself again. I am excited about the start of a new school year. There will be stress involved and I will have bad days, but it is different and better. Teaching is a hard job when you are mentally healthy and it is nearly impossible if you are not. Please, listen to your body, listen to your family, and make sure you take care of yourself, even if that means walking away for a while.

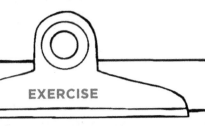

Learning to Cope with Stress

One of the first ways to start coping with our stress is to acknowledge it. What is causing stress for you? Are any of those stress triggers within your control to do something about? Finally, what approach do you want to take to address your stress and experience potential relief?

_____

_____

_____

_____

_____

_____

_____

_____

_____

_____

_____

_____

CHAPTER 16

IN CONTROL OR OUT OF CONTROL? WHICH IS IT?

When the conversation around growth mindsets started taking off in education, I was determined to make the concept more concrete and tangible for my students. This was important not only because the school considered it a priority but because I knew that individuals who demonstrated resilience often practiced a growth mindset. I, along with many other educators, hoped that this would become the mindset students carried forward with them in the coming years.

At the time, I had an elementary student who was incredibly gifted and had an abundant vocabulary. One day while out at recess, he came running up to me weighed down with very full pockets of rocks he had just collected from the playground. I asked him to share with me two of his favorite rocks and he pulled out one that was a milky quartz and another that was a jagged rock with sharp edges. He explained why these rocks would be added to his collection. The jagged rock with sharp edges had already been fractured on the weak points and created unique serrated and irregular edges. He then explained how he loves that rocks are rigid and don't really change a significant amount without a lot of force. There it was, the tangible example I was looking for.

With the help of this student and a few of the rocks from his collection, I gathered my students in a community circle to speak with them about a fixed mindset and a growth mindset. I shared that often we encounter moments in our day when things might feel a little challenging. When that happens, we need to stop and make a choice about how to meet that challenge. As we sat in the circle and passed around the rocks, we discussed how the rocks won't take on another shape or suddenly change. Then I pulled out some playdough and again passed it around the circle. By this point students were catching on and quickly noticed how the playdough could be shaped and changed into many different things. The playdough was flexible and could take on the shape of a rock, or it could be flattened, rolled up, or changed in other ways.

Our conversation led to how these objects reflect a fixed mindset and a growth mindset. The students recognized that when they were in a fixed mindset, a "rock brain," they were unwilling or unable to change. When they were thinking from their growth mindset, a flexible "playdough brain," they could develop their skills and understanding, even in the most challenging times, as long as they persevered and kept trying. This conversation carried over into the following days, and when preparing to teach students new information, I would hold up a rock and some playdough and ask them what we might need to get through the lesson. One of my absolute favorite moments was when a student asked if he could hold a piece of playdough to help him remember not to get stuck in his fixed mindset. To further reinforce the point, we created a T-chart that illustrated the connection between the different mindsets and the rock and the playdough.

Rocks and playdough, who knew they could offer so much?!

Throughout my years in education I continued to use this analogy with students again and again, but I started to notice how I was asking my students, and even myself, to consider having a flexible "playdough brain" when it came to things that were unexpected and often beyond our control. This was often the message I would leave for them on days when there would unexpectedly be a substitute teacher in the classroom. Would they choose to move through that day with a "rock brain" or a "flexible playdough brain" when they could experience something different or challenging but still find a way to go with the flow and do hard things?

> *"There are things in your life you can control—
> and there are variables you can't. The more
> diligent you are at controlling what you can, the
> more influence you'll have over your destiny.
> You just have to figure out which are which."*
>
> —Carleton Young, actor

When I feel overwhelmed with circumstances at work or in my personal life, I go back to that T-chart of a rock and playdough, and start to consider my circumstances and my choices. What is *out* of my control and cannot be changed or influenced, and what is *in* my control and can be changed or influenced?

This practice helps me identify where to focus the bulk of my energy (on the things I can influence) such as my routine, how I treat myself and others, my mindset, and the words I offer myself and others. Additionally, I identify what I can release myself from (the things I cannot control), such as traffic and weather, how others treat or perceive me, what a colleague chooses to prioritize, and the circumstances of challenging situations.

Along these lines, in *The 7 Habits of Highly Effective People,* Stephen Covey shares the concept of the circle of concern and influence. The circle of concern encompasses any concern you may have within your personal and professional life that you can actually do something about. Covey explains that proactive people are those who focus primarily on the concerns within their circle of influence.

In the book *Onward: Cultivating Emotional Resilience in Educators,* author Elena Aguilar describes a tool called the spheres of influence that she often uses when coaching her clients. The spheres of influence helps an individual consider and identify the following three areas: what the individual has control over, what the individual can influence, and what lies beyond their control and influence. By identifying and labeling concerns within these three spheres, it becomes easier to determine how the individual should respond and where to place their energy.

Perhaps you have a regular practice of considering what lies within your control and what remains out of your control, and if so, kudos to you. If you do not, consider implementing one using the exercise at the end of this chapter as a guideline.

A Personal Account of Building Resilience
—Mike W., 5th-grade teacher

Being a 5th-grade teacher is my dream job, which is remarkable considering that I "backed into" the teaching profession. When I began college, the one thing that I was sure of was that I didn't want to declare education as my major. My dad, brother, and sister were all in public education, and I wanted to etch my own path. Instead, I began my college career with two separate majors, health and exercise science and journalism. I was not a motivated student in these programs, as evidenced by my cumulative GPA. When I completed a semester in which I failed Introduction to Journalism but aced Ethical Journalism, my mom asked me what was next. "I guess I'll just go into education" escaped my lips, completely unintended. For the next three years, I was an honor roll student in elementary education. After that, I knew that I'd finally found the correct path to take.

It seems like there is always something new added to the plates of modern educators, while very little is ever removed. Current statistics show that half of all new teachers leave the profession within five years, which indicates that the demands of the profession are too often an overwhelming burden on its professionals. I feel like I am the exception and not the rule as a modern public school teacher, because I don't feel saddled by rising expectations and stressors. I know that these adverse conditions exist, yet I've found a way to mitigate their effects on my day-to-day experience. I feel guilty about my comfort compared to those who feel like their only option is to quit the profession. My case should not be the exception.

In other professions, workers can see the results of their efforts almost immediately. If I worked in a factory producing automotive parts, I could see the fruits of my labor lying on a surface in front of me, ready to be installed into a car right away. If I was a painter, I could step back from the canvas to see what I created. Teachers don't get to experience similar results. When the last hour of the last school day is completed, what we see in front of us is not a finished product. We merely pass these students on to the next level in their schooling. Since we can't attain the same immediate results as people in other professions, we have to celebrate the moments of growth and perseverance demonstrated by both our students and ourselves.

I celebrate the moments that aren't featured on student report cards. For example, when a student sticks with the learning process and learns how a mistake was made, when an "Aha!" moment indicates that a major hurdle in comprehension has just been cleared, or when a student commits to creating a new habit even though the process can be arduous. I also celebrate the moments that aren't featured on my teacher evaluation. For example, when I make a connection with a student that has nothing to do with academics but could help smooth out a difficult situation later on in the year, when I take a deep breath while looking at my handmade "Dignity and Respect" poster hanging in the room prior to an interaction with a student who's making bad choices, or when I witness students helping each other out because the classroom atmosphere promotes collaboration.

This is the "marathon and not a sprint" mentality put into action. I can thrive as a teacher when I can drift with the ebb and flow of the school year, and especially when I can teach my students to do the same. One blown assignment, lesson, or assessment does not mean that I am ineffective in my role, nor does it indicate that my students are incapable of grasping the content. I thrive as a teacher because I realize that the factors leading to success or failure are innumerable, and almost all of them are beyond my control. A student can be successful when they feel comfortable in the classroom. Period. I can create the atmosphere that promotes success, but every factor outside of the classroom is beyond my control.

Practice Using a Circle of Influence

Think of a stressful situation. Using the circle below, note which stress factors belong on the inside of the circle, and which ones belong outside of the circle. Does this type of exercise alleviate some of your stress load by helping you identify where to direct your energy?

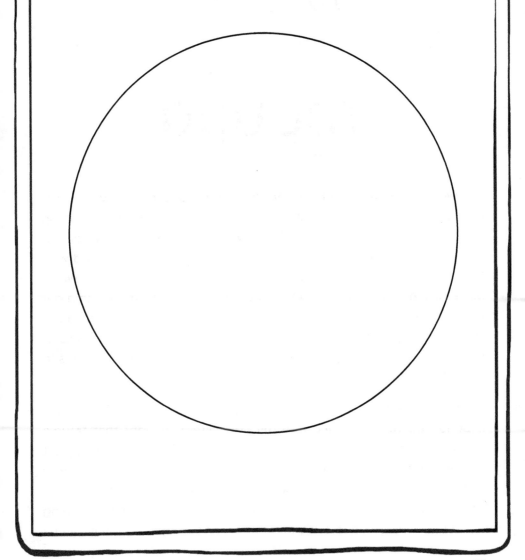

CHAPTER 17

WHAT IS TRAUMA, REALLY?

τραύμα

The word "trauma" is derived from the Greek concept of having a distinct physical or mental wound. Although this is an ancient concept, many professionals, including those who work directly with populations of people who have experienced trauma, are not equipped with the skills and knowledge necessary to support trauma in today's workplace. Trauma has a significant impact on what is going on within our classrooms for both students *and* teachers. By learning about the consequences of trauma, we can begin to foster a deeper awareness of why this is an urgent and relevant issue, especially one that pertains to educators all over the nation.

How does one know if they or their loved ones are experiencing or have experienced trauma? Long into my adult life, I thought that trauma was a term reserved for those who had experienced severe neglect and abuse, or had spent time in a war zone. While these occurrences can be traumatic, there are other variances of trauma that can occur from a single incident like a car accident or act of violence, ongoing experiences that lead to complex trauma, or even generational trauma from oppression and racism. When we consider that trauma is less about what happens to you and more about how you experience what happens to you, it takes on a much broader definition. Most likely, you or someone close to you has encountered an experience that at one point in time overwhelmed your system, whether your thoughts, emotions, or body, and impacted the way in which you perceived the world and moved through it. Trauma exposure can come from neglect, abuse, and war. However, it can also come from bullying, witnessing violence, experiencing an accident or natural disaster, having a medical emergency, and more. After having a traumatic experience, an individual may shift into a fight, flight, or freeze behavior. A damaged sense of safety can impact your ability to connect and relate to others. To begin to understand these challenges, it is essential to both evaluate the prevalence of trauma in your personal life, as well as in your students' lives.

> "Trauma is defined as anything that overwhelms our capacity to cope and leaves us feeling helpless, hopeless, or out of control."
> —Seane Corn,
> yoga teacher and activist

CHAPTER 18

TRAUMA IN THE CLASSROOM

"Trauma has become so commonplace that most people don't recognize its presence. Each of us has had a traumatic experience at some time in our lives, regardless of whether it left us with an obvious case of post-traumatic stress."

—Peter Levine, author of *Waking the Tiger: Healing Trauma*

Trauma is prevalent in our society, and in our classrooms. It is worth considering how we, along with our students, may be experiencing trauma from an increased frequency of disasters such as mass gun violence, poverty, family separation, displacement from natural disaster, and more recently, the COVID-19 virus. Humanitarian crises of many forms are becoming more and more frequent, greatly impacting the lives of students, yet only 2 percent of global humanitarian funding is dedicated to education.[22] In some districts, the effects of trauma are more severe than in others. Trauma-inducing crises are becoming increasingly more common, and education workers are feeling the strain from this reality. The issue of trauma in the classroom has become more important and complicated as the frequency of these crises increases. We know that trauma not only impacts behavior and learning, but our hearts, minds, and overall health as well.

Trauma and the Brain

"Being safe and feeling safe are not the same thing."

—Barry Svigals, educator and architect;
Sam Seidel, educator and author

The human brain is a complex system that requires multiple moving parts to operate in conjunction with one another to produce healthy cognitive processes. Essentially, there are three parts: the neocortex, limbic system, and reptilian brain.[23] Though they work together, each part has distinct responsibilities, and each can be impacted by traumatic experiences. There is a vast amount of literature on "lizard brain" thinking, a term used to describe when we, or our students, shift into a reptilian brain in which very little learning occurs.

During learning experiences, our brains consume roughly 20 percent of the body's energy.[24] For individuals experiencing vicarious trauma or chronic stress, this percentage is even greater. Have you ever noticed that your most disruptive students are also the ones who are moving around and fidgeting a lot? Taking breaks for movements, jumping, or standing can increase the brain's oxygen levels and help us function with more emotional regulation and awareness.

It is important to remember and distinguish that trauma is not something simply upsetting or disturbing. A traumatic experience impacts our internal chemistry, leaving an imprint on every level of our being. It influences the way in which we experience the world as well as our actions within it.

Trauma and Our Students

Childhood trauma is a public health issue.[25]

Trauma in an educational context can significantly affect the emotional, cognitive, and behavioral states of both children and adults. According to the Centers for Disease Control and Prevention (CDC), adverse childhood experiences, otherwise known as ACEs, are potentially traumatic events that occur in children between the ages of 0 to 17 years.[26] When children enter the classroom carrying high levels of stress from a traumatic experience, it has an impact on both their academics and their surrounding community. Some students may be traumatized by living in economically disadvantaged homes where they lack access to proper health care. Others may suffer from frequent disruptions in their home, a lack of educational resources, or even substandard housing. These disruptions may lead to students showing up in classrooms distracted by uncertainty, fear, and instability.

We may see specific signs or behaviors from a student who has experienced trauma presenting itself in the classroom. Trauma in children often manifests outwardly, affecting students' relationships and interactions. Signs of trauma may be seen in a student acting out in class, or in more subtle ways such as failure to make eye contact or repeatedly tapping a foot. Other signs of trauma include difficulty focusing, poor self-regulation, fatigue, anxious or fearful tendencies, feelings of guilt or shame, being easily startled, and more. Additionally, a student's trauma may manifest in behaviors such as hyperarousal and/or hypervigilance, avoidance and/or defiance, and potential struggles with development or attachment. These behaviors can significantly impact a student's ability to build relationships and feel safe enough to take risks and learn.

One third of the children living in our nation's urban neighborhoods suffer from PTSD (post-traumatic stress disorder) at nearly twice the rate reported for troops returning from war in Iraq.[27] Many educators have encountered the challenges involved with working with students with a history of trauma. Many of us have witnessed students dissociating, withdrawing, or acting out violently or aggressively. In our field we are encouraged to manage behaviors by focusing on the source, or root of the behavior, instead of the behavior itself. It is crucial for educators to remember that traumatized students are responding to stressful and overwhelming experiences that impair their ability to cope, or access important self-regulatory skills. Under-resourced communities are particularly challenged when basic needs are not being met. These situations deserve critical consideration because we know that schools provide several benefits beyond basic learning (shelter, adult care and affection, food, and play). It's because of this that attending school is crucial to relieving trauma.

When I was in college, I received no training on how to identify or support students experiencing a mental health "struggle." I received little information that adequately prepared me to respond to such challenges when presented by those in my care.

But that's okay, that's what counselors and social workers are for, right? Sure, but as funding is cut or decreased, we find fewer and fewer schools with a counselor and/or social worker to offer this vital support to both students and staff. Often these positions are spread thin with one individual servicing multiple schools or functioning at a student/adult ratio that is unsustainable, limiting their ability to be proactive rather than reactive. Student/teacher ratios continue to rise as districts make additional cuts and fewer teachers enter the profession. I've had the benefit of teaching in a district that maintained small class sizes, with my largest class reaching a maximum of 18. After my family moved, I began teaching in an urban district in which a class size of 18 was unheard of. How can a teacher create meaningful relationships with students when they average 30 students per class?

Yet educators work tirelessly to make it happen. They use their common sense, creativity, and empathy to connect with students in even the most overwhelming of situations. They work hard to do this for very little money and with very little money. They work hard to do this even when they are frustrated, stressed, and sleep deprived. They work hard to do this even when it begins to take a toll on their own feelings of safety and well-being, because they know the powerful impact a strong connection has on a student/teacher relationship.

The American Psychiatric Association defines Post-Traumatic Stress Disorder as: Lasting substantial effects on a person's psychosocial and somatic functioning that occurs from a single traumatizing event, or reoccurring exposure to neglect or abuse[28]

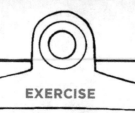
How to Work with a Traumatized Student

If we viewed a student's behavior as a form of communication, what might they be trying to communicate? It has been suggested that rather than asking what is wrong with a student, to consider what has happened to the student. Considering what your teachers did to help you feel safe and connected, how can you create a sense of safety and connection for your students?

_____

_____

_____

_____

_____

_____

_____

_____

_____

_____

_____

_____

_____

CHAPTER 19

THE ONGOING IMPACT OF ADVERSE CHILDHOOD EXPERIENCES

Adverse childhood experiences (ACEs) can have an impact that extends far beyond childhood. About 61 percent of adults report they have experienced at least one type of ACE, and nearly one in six have experienced four or more types of ACEs.[29] Not only do we see far-reaching implications of ACEs on one's health, but as these experiences continue to become more common, we begin to see how they impact multiple people in multiple communities in multiple ways. Many adults may be living with wounds that have not yet been addressed or healed. When the adult happens to be the educator in the room, their trauma may become triggered and played out again in schools with the children they are trying to protect and serve. We see these implications playing out in our communities and affecting systems that provide services in health, justice, and education. High-stress jobs lead to stressed-out individuals, and we know stress takes a toll. With the knowledge that these implications exist, we must choose to either turn a blind eye or create platforms that promote healing.

I know, heavy stuff, right? Take a deep breath, maybe another one. There is hope. Our adversity is not our destiny, nor is it the destiny of our students. We may not be able to prevent adversity and trauma from happening, but we can impact how we move through it. We can raise awareness about ACEs and trauma, consider how to prevent them, work toward community solutions, and promote safe, stable, and nurturing relationships and environments. When the environment feels safer, more compassionate, and connected, we tend to feel braver and we can begin to make shifts and actually learn.

This awareness magnifies the importance of caring for oneself as we navigate the disruptions of life. When classrooms are overcrowded, under-resourced, and used to support those in underprivileged situations, teaching becomes challenging. When we have educators who are stressed out, underpaid, and bear the responsibility of multiple professionals, in addition to overcrowded and under-resourced classrooms, we create a cyclical breeding ground for stress and trauma. Students coming into classrooms with high ACE scores cannot heal overnight. In fact, healing may take a year or more. Healing journeys take time. So, what can we do to support a student during their healing journey? Fortunately, there is a lot that we can offer, from creating routines to seeking additional support and resources. However, because resources and support can vary from school to school, creating a sense of calm becomes the most consistent support we can offer regardless of where we find ourselves.

CHAPTER 20

THE ROLE OF SOCIAL EMOTIONAL LEARNING

"If we want to produce dramatic impacts on the life outcomes of kids experiencing toxic stress, we have to transform the lives of adults caring for them."

—Victor Carrion, MD

Six years ago the word "trauma," let alone "trauma-informed practices," was rarely uttered within a school setting. Now educators are asked to attend professional development seminars and adjust classrooms and curriculum to better support students' needs that arise from trauma manifesting in the classroom. For the most part, trauma-informed care boils down to safety, connection, and regulation. Educators can offer trauma-informed care by creating a safe environment, establishing connections, and building relationships. Do you teach and support practices that promote emotional regulation?

There is a growing emphasis on teaching social emotional learning. Our students have more than just academic needs. Children encounter both social and emotional experiences as they navigate each day. Helping students learn how to navigate these social and emotional experiences is vital to preparing the next generation. Social emotional learning helps students better relate to one another. It also helps them move through new social experiences, by teaching them to observe and then make informed decisions about how to act based on these observations.

We also need to help educators recognize that they too have social and emotional needs, and how they tend to them directly impacts their students. Denying our own needs only sets us up to feel more overwhelmed, depleted, and frustrated. We cannot be there for our students if we aren't there for ourselves. Are you prioritizing and nurturing your own well-being? We need to be curious investigators, rather than individuals who act only on expectations and judgement. When we investigate a situation with curiosity rather than judgement, we take the time to ask what happened, rather than simply react when something goes wrong. When we do this, we can respond with more compassion.

How Charged Are You?

Have you ever reached the point at which you can no longer take on another thing without going over the edge? If so, you are not alone. This is a common feeling for many. In such cases, we often create a persona, swallow our truth, or push through rather than accept where we are in that moment. As humans, however, we all have limits.

How many of you have a cell phone? I was 23 years old when I got my first cell phone. I carried it around like it was my most prized possession. Over the past few years, when leading workshops for educators, I often ask participants to check the percentage of battery charge left on their cell phone. More often than not, very few participants have a battery charge of 50 percent or less. I'll then ask participants to consider the last time they engaged in an activity that aided in supporting their well-being. Did they do something that morning, within the past 24 hours, or within the past week? It's interesting isn't it? We seem to take care of our cell phones better than we take care of ourselves. We can't imagine going multiple days in a row without charging our cell phone to full capacity, and yet, we push ourselves to go multiple days, weeks, months, or even years without recharging. We would not expect our cell phone charge to last weeks or months before needing a charge. See the irony here?

Just in case you need to hear this, you have permission to take care of recharging yourself. You have permission to act before you are at zero percent with nothing left to give. Approach yourself proactively rather than reactively. You will find that what you need when you are at 25 percent looks very different from what you need when you are functioning at 75 percent. Regardless of where you find yourself, it is never too early to check in and recharge. You are the only version of you that you've got. Treat yourself like your most prized possession!

A Personal Account of Building Resilience

—Kim R., learning experience coordinator

As a science teacher, I have always been drawn to analogies to demonstrate scientific concepts. There were several moments in my teaching career when I was teaching a concept and the lightbulb would turn on. I would think of a way to make a connection between science and my everyday life. I would then jot down these ideas in my planner. My lesson plan books are lined with tips like "Hippos can't jump and energy is transferred."

One such analogy that sticks with me is the concept of endothermic and exothermic reactions as they relate to the teaching profession. Bear with me here as I give a brief explanation of each concept.

Exothermic reactions transfer energy outward to the surroundings. They are a release of energy, usually in the form of heat. In order for this reaction to occur, bonds must be formed. This type of reaction causes the surroundings to warm up, as the energy is transferred outward. The energy comes from the reactants and flows outward so the energy in the reactants decreases over the course of the reaction. These reactions are common in nature.

Endothermic reactions take in energy from the surroundings. They are an absorption of energy, usually in the form of heat. In order for this reaction to occur, bonds have to be broken. This type of reaction causes the surroundings to cool down, as energy is transferred inward. Additional energy, or activation energy, is required for these reactions to occur. So energy is added to the system and remains after the reaction occurs. These reactions are less common in nature.

This analogy speaks to teaching and maintaining the ability to do so effectively. Teaching is an exothermic reaction. Teachers transfer energy outward to their students. They explain concepts, exude love, and reveal a depth of passion for the subject matter. Teaching requires energy at the start, in the reactants, teacher, and students. The hope is that students "catch" the energy and the heat in the room builds and it gets hot! Relational bonds must be created for this to happen in a classroom. Every teacher has had the thrill of a figurative fire starting in their classrooms as students get excited about their learning. The energy is palpable and addicting. Effective educators do this multiple times a day, every day of the week. That is a lot of energy. It is no wonder that teachers are beat by lunch time.

That is where endothermic reactions factor into the equation. In order for this work to be done, teachers have to absorb energy from somewhere. We, as educators, have to break down bonds in order to take in this energy. The bonds of bias and doubt, and the bonds that tell us rest is for the weak. Endothermic reactions increase our energy so we have it to give the next day or the next class period. Teachers find these energy sources in other like-minded educators, exercise (although the analogy breaks down as this is an exothermic reaction), meditation, deep breathing, hydrating, listening to music, closing our eyes, being in nature, being creative, or just taking a break.

My teaching is at its best after a summer or a mid-year break. I spend that time pulling energy into myself, through my family, my hobbies, and my talents. I have saturated myself with these life-giving activities, and it is stored for later use.

I also know the dreaded month of February when I have been burning exothermically for two solid months and have barely caught my breath. It is hot but not in the way described above. It is hot in short fuses and in despair, all of which flow outward as well. Burnout is real for teachers and students.

The demands of the classroom are not lessening. In my 13 years of teaching, the amount of exothermic reactions I have been called to do is continually increasing. So, the required endothermic reactions I engage in are essential for my effectiveness and well-being. This is a lesson I have had to learn by burning to my core. It isn't pretty. I have had days when a cry in the parking lot was the wakeup call I needed. I have hugged coworkers as they struggled to make it to the end of the day, with the hope that I could syphon energy to them, so they could make it through the day.

I have debated leaving the profession in hope of rescuing myself from the abusive relationship that teaching can be if balance is not found.

The outward transfer of energy is hard, but kindling the fire of a student's love of learning is powerful.

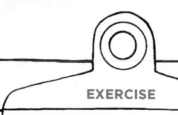

Recharging Your Energy

We all encounter circumstances that drain our energy. Where do you get your energy? What helps you feel recharged? How can you add such moments of recharge throughout your day?

_____

_____

_____

_____

_____

_____

_____

_____

_____

_____

_____

_____

_____

_____

CHAPTER 21

EDUCATORS AND VICARIOUS TRAUMA

"Nothing can be changed until it is faced."

—James Baldwin

As educators, we often feel we have a responsibility to "take the temperature of the room" and then respond accordingly. Initially, we function as a thermometer, taking the current temperature of the room and anticipating what might follow. Then, we make a shift and become the thermostat working to regulate the environment, preventing it from becoming "too hot or too cold." This translates into the classroom when we attempt to manage the atmosphere—the behaviors, culture, energy, and emotions of each individual in the room.

The term "first responders" is associated with those working with the public in ways that are life-altering or lifesaving, such as in the fields of law enforcement, fire-fighting, and emergency medical services. Educators should also be recognized as first responders since they also impact the public in ways that are life-altering or lifesaving. Educators are directly involved with the lives of so many who are in need of care and support. We serve a vital role as first responders, especially to our students with trauma. Unfortunately, it is not uncommon for educators to overlook their own basic needs, even more so while experiencing chronic stress, burnout, compassion fatigue, or vicarious trauma. But empathy does not have to come at the cost of an educator's well-being.

One third of the current adult population has experienced significant adverse traumatic events.[30] We know that the brain is impacted by distressing experiences, which can lead to certain habits, attitudes, or mental health issues. Such is the case for those working with student populations that are experiencing trauma. Professionals working in these fields do not necessarily receive training on how to prevent burnout, compassion fatigue, or vicarious trauma.

Experiencing a state of physical or emotional exhaustion, which leads to constantly feeling drained or unable to cope, is known as burnout. Although the term has been used since the 1980s, it wasn't until 2019 that workplace burnout became an official diagnosis recognized by the World Health Organization. According to the National Child Traumatic Stress Network, compassion fatigue is "the emotional duress that results when an individual hears about the first-hand trauma experiences of another." When we experience compassion fatigue, it is more difficult to offer compassion and empathy to those around us. Any educator who works directly with traumatized children and adolescents is vulnerable to the effects of burnout and compassion fatigue. Vicarious trauma, also known as secondary trauma, occurs when there is moral distress or when one is feeling overwhelmed by repeated exposure to students' traumas.

When immersed in a career in education, it is not uncommon to experience vicarious trauma. Hearing the stories of our students, their families, and the people in our communities, we become hypervigilant in our surroundings, constantly scanning for any potential threats, all while managing our endless efforts to do this important, hard work.

Vicarious trauma is often experienced by caregivers and first responders who are witness to the pain, fear, and terror others experience. Such individuals are traumatized through the experience of another person. The best way to deal with compassion fatigue and vicarious trauma is early recognition. Who is the most vulnerable? Those who work directly with children, those who experience high levels of stress, those who are empathetic, those who help others, and those who have experienced trauma in their own lives. Symptoms of vicarious trauma include difficulty focusing, appetite changes, anger and/or sadness, isolation, depression, aggression, anxiety, or insomnia. An individual doesn't have to check all of the boxes to be experiencing vicarious trauma. Nor does it mean that if you have one of the symptoms, you are experiencing vicarious trauma.

Burnout, compassion fatigue, and vicarious trauma create huge challenges for educators. As such, we need to have a greater understanding of how this kind of stress and trauma affects the brain and body. As individuals working with others in a high-stress environment, it is imperative we become aware of how different life experiences impact us and trigger certain responses. Once we learn to recognize and identify our triggers, we can manage our responses by asking the following:

- What do I need to do to self-regulate? Should I take a few deep breaths or do I need to let something go?
- What can I do to bring myself back to feeling safe?
- How can I reconnect to myself and those around me?

If you think that you may be experiencing chronic stress, burnout, compassion fatigue, or even vicarious trauma, I highly encourage you to express your concern to those around you, the ones you trust. Check in with them on a daily basis by sharing your concerns and asking if they've noticed anything. Then reach out to a professional, whether a coach, a therapist, or a physician, to help you make a recovery plan. Remember, you deserve the same love and care you offer so many others. You matter, too.

There may be a correlation between the rise of trauma and vicarious trauma in the classroom, and the rise of teacher turnover rates in our nation. Perhaps a doctoral student will explore this potential correlation. Regardless, experiencing vicarious trauma and teaching burnout creates additional challenges and pressures on top of an already demanding and emotionally exhausting career. This may not be the sole reason for teacher turnover, but it is likely that the pressure created within this environment can lead those in education to leave the profession. Working in such conditions may lead to feelings of being overwhelmed, incompetent, and inadequately supported.

A Personal Account of Building Resilience

—Colleen W., ELD program specialist and assistant principal

My journey as an educator began in high school during a career counseling session. The career counseling evaluation determined that I had strengths and interests that would allow me to be a social worker. I knew that would be a painful career choice for me because I am the type of person who holds onto worry, who deeply feels the pain of others, and who hates to feel powerless when I feel as though I should be able to protect people. Even as a 17-year-old, I made a choice to care for my soul. Somewhere along the path of my educational career, I forgot how to do that and how essential it is.

I became a teacher so I could make the world a better place by building up young children. I wanted to influence the world through future generations by showing them love and how to be curious and ask questions. My work with children in elementary schools continues to be fulfilling. I delight in seeing the world through their eyes—tiny perseverant optimists, full of joy at every new experience.

It was in my first year of teaching that I realized seeing the world through my students' eyes was joyful, at times, but at other times painful. I came to see the world as being sometimes cruel and unfair to our youngest members of society. While many of my students lived wonderfully privileged lives, many did not. Those were the stories that followed me home again and again. Being the first to uncover abuse and neglect, knowing about the harsh words spoken to a child first thing in the morning, seeing children who are scared to go home, hearing children calling me mom because they "wished I was their mom"—all of this was utterly painful. My heart became weighed down by their experiences, and it felt like a heavy weight to bear. I felt anger and pain over the loss of innocence in so many childhoods. I thought back on my own childhood many times and wished for the opportunity to provide even a simple, small piece of that for so many of my students.

I could not solve or fix these situations easily. My continuous concern for my students had started to impact me, and I experienced what

I imagine many teachers do. I worried. I lost sleep because I would wake up full of anxiety about what my students might be experiencing. When I was sleeping, I would grind my teeth and clench my jaw to the point that my once-straight smile became quite crooked. I would sleepwalk, counting my kindergarten students in my bedroom, just to make sure that in my dreams, they were all there with me and safe. I wondered what was happening in my students' lives while being a loving mom to my son. I felt disheartened and disempowered as an educator because I felt that I truly could not make things better for my students in the ways that they needed and deserved. Little did I know that my continuous concern for my students would impact me in such significant ways.

Vicarious trauma is real, but I didn't learn about it until I was already starting to experience it. Vicarious trauma prevented me from being my best for my family and my students. It placed me in a state where I was constantly experiencing stress and worry. I would find myself wrapped up in anxious thoughts often brought on by even the simplest of things. I would see someone walking down the street in a neighborhood, and suddenly that made me think of the murders in Newtown, CT, and how that may happen again without any warning. I would worry about health and sickness to the point that I was impacting my own health, and I began to experience panic attacks.

As an assistant principal, I see this all too often with the teachers I support. The stories their students share with them wear heavy on their faces when we talk and their hearts are hurting. It was not until I realized that I needed to be an example to my colleagues, to this amazing team that I lead, that I explored my own healing. Thankfully, our school district employs a counseling team for staff, and a few sessions are included at no cost in our benefits package. When necessary, they can refer us for more sessions or additional care as needed. I met with a counselor for nearly a year to discuss my anxiety, how it was impacting my life, and how I could gain control over my racing mind. She suggested meditation as an additional tool to add to my self-care routine, which previously consisted of yoga and time spent in the outdoors. Adding mediation to the mix helped me to more fully find and experience peace in both of these healing practices.

Meditation has also helped me quiet the chaos. It has allowed me to focus on what is happening in the present moment as well as what lives in my sphere of influence. I was empowered simply by being able to control my breath in an anxiety-inducing situation. While resting into a long pose during a restorative yoga session, the teacher said to "let the earth hold you...rest into the earth." That simple idea took a weight off of me. I didn't have to carry the world, instead I could lean into it and my own inner strength.

My sense of empowerment, while still in need of nurturing, has grown. It allows me to be more calm, present, and thoughtful in times of high stress and pain. Finding my breath and becoming more grounded by this simple thing, this simple thing that lives within me everywhere I go in every moment, allows me to be a light because I have the mental space free to fully do so. It is hard to sit in stillness at first. But the stillness begins to empower and nurture through every moment in life, and you can bring that with you as an advocate for those in need of stillness and grounding themselves.

Exploring Your Knowledge of Burnout, Compassion Fatigue, and Trauma

When did you first hear of the terms "compassion fatigue" or "vicarious trauma"? Have you experienced burnout, compassion fatigue, and/or vicarious trauma in the workplace? Does any of the above information resonate with you? Finally, what emotions do you notice in response to reading about it?

_____

_____

_____

_____

_____

_____

_____

_____

_____

_____

_____

_____

CHAPTER 22

WIDENING OUR WINDOWS OF TOLERANCE

Educators on the "front lines" act as the first responders to everything that occurs within their communities, whether it be violence, pandemics, natural disasters, or the ongoing systems that perpetuate racism. This is a heavy burden to bear. Yet, time and time again, educators are asked to meet, overcome, and solve any challenges that come their way in the classroom. It is unfair to expect this from them without having someone or something available to help ease the burden they carry. To help ease that burden, educators must learn to either become superhumans or expand their resilience.

Dr. Dan Siegel coined the term "window of tolerance," which is used to describe a space of optimal arousal, when we feel and do our best. There are times we will get bumped out of this space, but the goal is to return to the middle, the place where we can be more fully present and function in an optimal state of well-being.

Without a deep sense of awareness and understanding of ourselves, we are blind to the things that trigger us or push us to our limits or even over the edge. When educators, who are often caring, nurturing and empathetic individuals, work with students who are experiencing high levels of stress, it is natural that we will absorb some of that stress. We can temporarily take on the stress and trauma of another individual, but that doesn't mean that we need to carry it forever.

A Personal Account of Building Resilience

—Lillian H., high school English teacher

To promote my resiliency, I attempt to eat healthy, get enough sleep, exercise, allow for personal and family time, get massages, say no to extra things at work, say no to volunteering at church or my kids' school, see a psychologist/therapist regularly, and make sure I practice meditation. Despite all of this, after I had my baby and returned to work, I found myself occasionally curled up in a ball under my desk sobbing after leaving a staff meeting in which we were told that once again, we would have to do more with even less. I resent that the resilience of an educator seems to solely be the responsibility of the educator. I feel as if I am being told that the stress I am experiencing is somehow my fault for not doing the exact "right" mental health strategies, and that is why I am unable to handle being an educator. I call this BS. When do the administrators and systems at play take responsibility for my mental health? I will never return to teaching full-time unless tragedy strikes and it is my only option. All teachers should walk out of the classroom and not come back until changes happen, but we won't because we know it impacts children. It's not our fault for not figuring out the exact "right way" of how to improve our mental health on top of everything else we constantly have thrown our way.

One of the most important goals, while considering a commitment to self-care, is to increase one's tolerance for adversity. By becoming aware of our personal tolerance for stressful and overstimulating situations, we become more aware of what triggers us and pushes us out of our optimal state, in addition to becoming more effective at widening our window of tolerance and returning to an optimal state.

We need to become keenly aware of how to offer ourselves the care and repair needed to develop resiliency "muscles" so we can continue doing the important work of educating our students. If we do not, we run the risk of shifting into compassion fatigue, burnout, and vicarious trauma. To avoid this, we need to learn how to view the world through trauma-informed and resilience-focused lenses. If you are worried it's too late, don't be discouraged because there is still hope. No matter how deeply worn the paths are in regard to our habits and ways of caring for ourselves, we have the ability to create new ones. We'll dive more into developing and maintaining resiliency in Part 3.

PART III
Rising Resilient

CHAPTER 23

PRIORITIZING OUR WELL-BEING

"To have well-being you must have resilience."

—Dr. Rick Hanson

The invitation to connect and collaborate with educators and engage in conversations that can reduce the burnout so many are experiencing is long overdue. Teacher meetings tend to focus on the current goals of the administration, the curriculum, or student behavior rather than on how experiences in the classroom impact faculty. We don't really allow for such discussions until the end of the year, at which point many educators no longer have the capacity to have such conversations in a constructive and helpful manner, because they are already maxed out.

What message do we send to educators about prioritizing their well-being when it is an afterthought in the ongoing conversation? Most people in our society want educators to continue to do this good, important work. Unfortunately, we don't give them the tools they need to help them prioritize their well-being so they can continue to do just that. Who is there to help ensure that the teachers who are taking care of so many are being taken care of themselves?

Throughout my lifetime, I have encountered more than one scenario where I thought, "If I can just wait until _____." Or, "This will be so much easier when I_____." In fact, as I was in the process of writing this book,

I would set aside time regularly to commit to writing. It seemed that more often than not, on those days, some disruption would interrupt the time I had set aside specifically for writing. This also happened while working in the classroom. Something else will always demand more of my time and attention. These experiences can be frustrating and leave me feeling discouraged about the progress, or lack thereof, that I am making. However, life doesn't stop when we have deadlines or heavy workloads, but it sure would be nice if it did. But here is the thing, we can't wait. We can't wait until all of the tasks on the to-do list are completed, we've made it to the next school break, or until after this pandemic, to start caring for ourselves and putting into place practices that build resilience.

As I was encountering interruption after interruption, I decided to prioritize some time and set aside two weeks to minimize interruptions and maximize putting content on paper. The day before that two-week window, life was significantly disrupted by the COVID-19 pandemic. School was canceled and shelter-in-place orders were issued. Those two weeks now consisted of a house full of family members, and even more uncertainty and emotions to navigate.

I would love to tell you that things suddenly fell into place, but they did not.

Instead, I had to up my game because all of these new circumstances required more of my time and attention mentally and emotionally. To preserve and prioritize resilience, I had to utilize more reflective practices to help me process my thoughts and emotions so I could respond with care and compassion to my needs and the needs of those around me. Practices such as mindfulness, yoga, and movement helped me regulate and build my capacity for dealing with challenging and unforeseeable situations. I had to keep connecting, not just with myself, but with the larger collective I am a part of, to keep going.

I tried to commit the first two hours of my day to prioritizing these practices so when I experienced some form of disruption, stress, or strain during the day, it didn't take me as long to recover. I didn't always have the time or energy to give two full hours before the day began, so I would pick and choose another point in the day to fit it in.

This wasn't easy to do, but I knew it was essential. Sometimes I could make this happen, and other times it was a struggle. However, setting this priority helped me move forward because I felt like I was choosing how to spend my time rather than having circumstances choose for me. By prioritizing my well-being, I had a deeper sense of awareness regarding my needs and limits, which allowed for more of my complete attention to be given to writing when time allowed.

Fortunately, human beings have the capacity to overcome stressful or traumatic experiences. No matter how deeply worn the paths in regard to our habits, we have the ability to create new ones. Neuroplasticity is the scientific notion that describes the brain's ability to create new neural pathways and "rewire" itself. Knowing that our thoughts, actions, and routines can physically alter our brain gives tremendous hope for our work on developing and maintaining resiliency.

Now, more than ever, we need practices that develop and maintain our resilience. We shouldn't wait until we've reached a crisis to start tending to our well-being and practicing acts of care that build resilience. We need to make care and repair a priority in order to sustain a healthier state of well-being. Much like other areas of our life, we won't set a goal and suddenly wake up the next day having met that goal. No one decides to run a marathon without putting in the long hours of training first. But it can no longer be an option for us. It is a necessity. I am asking you to prioritize your ability to be more resilient.

"Resilience is not just for surviving the worst day of your life. It's for thriving every day of your life."

—Dr. Rick Hanson

Building Resilience

What practices help you preserve and prioritize resilience? How do these practices help you move through challenging moments or days? Is there anything you can do to become more resilient?

_____

_____

_____

_____

_____

_____

_____

_____

_____

_____

_____

_____

CHAPTER 24

THE MISCONCEPTIONS ABOUT RESILIENCE

*"Stamina is one part of resilience
or grit. Bravery is another."*

—Jena Pincott, author of *Wits, Guts, Grit*

Resiliency is not a common topic of conversation in lunchrooms or teacher lounges. Over the years as I gained a greater appreciation for the importance of resiliency in my own life, I started to ask colleagues to explain their understanding of what it means to be resilient. I was surprised at how many define resilience in a way that disregards personal well-being. Rather, they define resilience by using the word "grit" and describing it as one's ability to tolerate everything that comes their way, regardless of how difficult the circumstances may be, and to keep going no matter what. Essentially they equated grit to perseverance. But being resilient does *not* mean that we grin and bear our way through every circumstance or have complete disregard for ourselves. Resilience should not be a painful punishment that we simply endure as we soldier on.

So what is resilience, and how can we get it? Some refer to resilience as the ability to bounce back and return to a state of normalcy. While this may be true to a certain degree, we will encounter some experiences throughout our lifetime that we cannot just bounce back from due to the long-term impact of some catastrophic events. Resilience is not an absence of pain, struggle, or hardship. In fact, resilience is more about how you cultivate strength to move through and cope with setbacks, obstacles, or barriers.

While I do think that resilience is in part demonstrated when we keep going or persevere, especially during difficult circumstances, I do not think it means we must push ourselves through unbearable pain in order to persevere. When we view resilience in this manner, we set ourselves up to feel trapped, hopeless, and helpless. It's because of this mentality that some individuals think resilience is demonstrated by:

- Getting up and going to work each day, even when feeling physically, emotionally, and mentally exhausted, and repeating this action five days a week.

- Not complaining about circumstances, even when faced with seemingly insurmountable obstacles.

- Showing up with a smile and surviving whatever comes your way despite all of the challenges, the heavy workload, and continuing to put the needs of others above your own at all times.

To me, that mentality seems more like the "dark side of resilience,"[31] a term used by Tomas Chamorro-Premuzic and Derek Lusk, when something becomes more harmful than good. We are holding ourselves to unrealistic expectations and standards if we think of a resilient individual as one who never needs to step away, doesn't give up, and doesn't get overwhelmed by stress or trauma. I worry that in this mindset, we are setting ourselves up for a lack of compassion and support. We need to leave room for the belief that stepping back isn't necessarily failure but instead a courageous act of care. Would we expect the same from our students? Do we expect our students to endure and keep going regardless of the struggle or hardship they encounter?

Our resilience has limits, and it's okay to have limits. We can't always do it all. It's okay to ask for help and take a break along the way when dealing with difficult things so that we can keep coming back. This is where courage comes in and plays a vital role in building and practicing resilience. We have to be brave enough to acknowledge our humanity. Let's lead with the example that we have limits and even with limits, we still have the ability to thrive.

CHAPTER 25

INCREASING YOUR RESILIENCY

"We create transformative, resilient new realities by becoming transformed, resilient people."

—Krista Tippett, journalist

Being an educator is hard work. There will be days when you feel over-whelmed and overworked. You might even find yourself wanting to walk away from it all. Resilience helps us thrive even in the midst of a struggle and constant change. Practicing resiliency is not going to be easy, nor will it allow you to control every circumstance you encounter. But resiliency will help you determine how you approach each circum-stance and challenge.

To increase resilience, we must first understand it and then practice it again and again. Resilience resides within all of us, and its presence within our lives often depends on how we cultivate and nurture it over the course of our lifetime. Another piece of good news, we never reach a point where it is no longer accessible to us. However, it may become harder to attain if we do not engage in practices that aid in building resilience on a regular basis. We are the CEO of our well-being. We decide our amount of resiliency by choosing to cultivate it or letting things lie stagnant and becoming disengaged.

"It's highly distressing to carry with you fear, pain, and uncertainty. But it's even more distressing trying to repress or forget those feelings. Resilience is not about bouncing back. It's about moving forward."

—Brad Stulberg, author of *Peak Performance:
Elevate Your Game, Avoid Burnout, and
Thrive with the New Science of Success*

Educators are role models. Let's model a resilient mindset by viewing challenges as opportunities for growth. Let's be models who demonstrate healthy coping strategies, make it safe to admit vulnerability and personal limitations, reject the stigma associated with imperfection, and be strong people who seek support and guidance.[32]

Think of one situation or experience in your life when you had to cultivate resilience. What did that time look like for you? As you recall this time, do you notice any shifts in your thoughts or feelings, maybe even in your body? How did you cultivate resilience during this time? Are any of those things present in your current day-to-day life?

Individual Resilience

We can think of resilience in two different ways: how we experience it as an individual, and how we experience it as a collective or a community. While there is some overlap in both of these experiences, there are also some distinct differences in what we encounter and create during each scenario. Largely, practices of individual resilience have to do with exactly that, you the individual and how your thoughts and behaviors, and the actions you take, nurture your personal well-being. No individual will move through life without encountering some problem or struggle along the way. A resilient individual recognizes that shifting into catastrophic thinking prevents them from growing through the struggle. These practices of resilience are centered around how you show up and hold space for yourself when encountering such events.

Community Resilience

Connection to and with others is a key part of resilience. Humans are hardwired for relationships. In "Building the Foundation of Learning Partnerships," author and educator Zaretta Hammond states that "in a collectivist, community-based culture, relationships are the foundation of all social, political, and cognitive endeavors." Our sense of connection to others occurs in different ways, whether it be found within a school or sports group, a civic group, or even a religious group. Each of these groups, especially when built upon trusting relationships that make us feel safe and secure, creates a sense of connection and belonging, which helps us to thrive and reach our full potential.

Interpersonal neurobiology is an interdisciplinary field that combines research from psychology, sociology, and cognitive science, among others, to better understand the function and importance of empathy and relationships within the human experience. At the forefront of this specialized field is Daniel J. Siegel, MD. His research is meant to challenge us to think about the concepts of compassion and kindness as not just helping those who are suffering, but actually helping people to flourish.[33] Our modern-day society has conditioned us to keep our schedules full and move through our days at the pace of a bullet train. In the workplace, it's easy to find ourselves too busy or too stressed, and often disconnected socially from our colleagues and associates.

Interpersonal neurobiology teaches us that our interpersonal relationships, how we connect with those in our community, influences our neurobiology, or our neurological and biological responses. In other words, what happens to us affects what happens in us.

Just like we know that stress can be contagious, joy, peace, and a sense of security can be contagious, too!

Relationships

Relationships matter. They matter with our students and their parents, the staff we work alongside, and our family members, and they play an important part in our health and well-being, especially when we build meaningful relationships built upon trust.

That connection we feel with our students, loved ones, and even our surroundings is often correlated to the connection we have with ourselves. We have to begin by having a deep relationship with ourselves.

Educator Support Circles

Somehow, even when surrounded by many people, the work of educating can feel isolating and lonely. When we are in a constant state of high stress, it begins to impact our relationships. It is challenging to connect emotionally when you are stressed out and without a sense of safety. That is why in trauma-informed practices, we often talk about creating a sense of safety to help foster and build relationships and connections.

One way that we can build connective relationships to experience community resilience is through a circle practice. This form of collective engagement derives from traditions found among indigenous communities around the world. There are a variety of ways that we implement a circle practice in our classrooms, whether during a morning meeting, an afternoon community circle, or in the context of a closing or restorative circle. "Circle sharing is a more formal way of practicing our deep listening and loving speech with others to open up about our thoughts and feelings."[34] Just like our students, educators need and deserve a space like this. Some of my fondest memories with colleagues occurred when I had the honor of facilitating these spaces. Within these spaces we have the opportunity to feel and experience connection, compassion, empathy, and support, and we are given the opportunity to offer it in return. We can breathe deeply together, and be a witness for one another, as we release some of the pain that comes with doing this work. By offering a space that provides deep listening and the opportunity to take care of one another, we potentially offer a space that brings healing. A community's ability to sustain, respond, and recover in response to a challenge is based on its capacity to show up in a healthy way.

A Personal Account of Building Resilience

—Ben S., kindergarten teacher

As an educator, you witness some of the very best things in life, and some of the worst. It is important to understand how your job impacts you and to know how to best care for yourself in a way that rejuvenates you so that each morning you can take on whatever the world has to throw at you. I, Mr. S., a 6'10", openly gay kindergarten teacher, have worked hard to find the ways that I can tend to myself to ensure that I am the best I can be, not only for myself, but also for my students and those around me.

My practices of self-care certainly look similar to some, but a little different from others in the workplace. Of course, there are things like a manicure or pedicure, getting my hair cut, or an evening walk that help to "fill my bucket," but in all honesty, most of my self-care is reliant on relationships. I always tell people that I went into education because of a TED Talk. Rita Pierson, a lifelong educator and educational coach, gave a TED Talk called "Every Kid Needs a Champion," where she highlights the "value and importance of human connection: relationships." Nothing has ever struck a chord in me like this woman's wise words, and until seeing her video, I had no way to accurately tell myself how to best tend to myself and my needs.

I am as extroverted as they come and frequently spend my time contemplating the shapes I see in the clouds, and consistently get way too excited about literally everything. I would not change this for anything. I largely depend on other people and my interactions with them to fill me up. Over time, I noticed the bulk of my self-care completely revolves around time spent in three significant relationships in my life—the relationships I have with my students, my teaching team, and my family (both chosen and given). These relationships give me the strength and determination to be the best version of myself.

If you talk to anyone who has been in the education world, you will hear wildly different stories, struggles, and triumphs. The one commonality is that the students are often the reason they show up and stay. Teaching is hard, but the students completely make the hard job worthwhile. For me, this is wildly true—my students do more than make my job worth staying in. If we break down my 24-hour day into an average timeline, I spend 8 hours, or 33% of my day at home sleeping. The remaining 67% of the time is spent, as Rita Pierson says, "either at the schoolhouse, on the way to the schoolhouse, or talking about what happened in the schoolhouse." Seeing as how I spend 8 hours of my day with my students, naturally they became an integral part of my self-care. There are few things better than kindergarteners being so overjoyed with how well they are writing their name or how excited they are that their dog barked that morning (yes, everything is exciting to them). As a teacher, rough things happen during the day, so I rely on the joy my students bring each day to help find and offer joy and happiness to them in return. How is it then not natural to see their joy and feel joy as well? They bring all of their joys and sorrows to the classroom and trust you, the teacher, enough to share it all with you.

When I am not educating my students, I am working with a superb group of fellow educators. Six of us make up the team that teaches the kindergarteners and 1st graders. I can confidently say that I wouldn't have made it through my second year of teaching without these wonderful friends. Feeling love and trust are crucial, and my team not only shows this to me, but they also provide support and understanding. Although one would think that teaching 5-, 6-, and 7-year-olds is all sunshine and roses, in reality it can be some of the hardest work you will ever do. You cannot go through this job without a solid support system in and out of school, and I am lucky enough to have teammates who offer me exactly that. We laugh, cry, problem solve, and share bits and pieces of our lives, all while helping each other through the many frustrations and hardships that come within and out of our jobs. These individuals impact me not only professionally, but personally and are a vital piece in my sense of connection and care.

The final piece of my self-care routine is perhaps the most important, but most delicate one of all. My family goes beyond nuclear and extends to individuals who make me feel completely whole and loved. I have been blessed with a wonderful, supportive family who truly wishes nothing but the best for me. I feel a bit boastful saying this, as this is not always the case with individuals in the world today, but it is true. In addition to my biological family, I have several individuals in my life that I consider to be like family. I laugh at myself a lot when I talk to people about my friends because I often reference someone as a "best friend" and a few sentences later find myself talking about another "best friend." This extensive list of best friends is an invaluable part of the glue that holds me together, and an even more cherished part of my self-care. My family, both chosen and given, help to not only bring love, trust, support, and understanding into my life, but they add happiness, devotion, kindness, and patience into the mix. Without them, I would truly be lost.

When I said before that my self-care was different from others, it's because I believe self-care is what you need to not only feel grounded, but also rejuvenated—it's what fills *your* cup, and it varies from individual to individual. My self-care is largely reliant on other people, because what grounds me, what rejuvenates me, is being surrounded by the people that I love and care for, and that love me in return. On some of my worst days of teaching or life in general, it is the people I mentioned in the paragraphs above that brought me back to being a better and even more ready version of myself.

Deepening Our Relationships

We need to be in a deep relationship with ourselves in order to have deep relationships with others. Consider the ways in which you connect with your students, colleagues, and those outside of your workplace. Do these connections come naturally, or do they take effort? If you were to reflect on the relationships you have, who uplifts you and brings you joy, gives you strength, or helps you prioritize your health? Who helps you navigate your most challenging times? Which relationships make you who you are? By bringing these individuals to mind, you invite the opportunity to experience a shift in the sensations of your well-being.

_____

_____

_____

_____

_____

_____

_____

_____

_____

CHAPTER 26

RESILIENCE BEGINS WITH SELF-AWARENESS

So, how do we nurture resilience, especially during these challenging times?

Resilience begins with self-awareness. One way to increase self-awareness is to spend time paying attention to yourself. My guess is that you spend a lot of time paying attention to everything but yourself.

Be honest, how often do you pay attention to yourself? Do you ever get to the end of the work day and realize that you haven't finished your morning coffee, or taken time to eat or even use the bathroom? It can be challenging to pay attention to ourselves, especially when there is so much to get through in a day. But we owe it to ourselves to be aware of our own needs.

The Collaborative for Academic, Social, and Emotional Learning (CASEL) focuses on increasing knowledge about social and emotional learning. According to CASEL, self-awareness is "the ability to accurately recognize one's own emotions, thoughts, and values and how they influence behavior. The ability to accurately assess one's strengths and limitations, with a well-grounded sense of confidence, optimism, and a growth mindset.[35]

We assess students on a continual basis to gain a better understanding of their needs and/or gaps in understanding. We need to develop a similar "assessment" regimen for ourselves to build a greater understanding of our own needs. If you were to collect data on yourself, what would it reveal? For example, it is important to know the factors that increase your stress levels. It also helps to remember what led you to a career in education. Such awareness helps you understand what motivates you, and what you value. Such knowledge allows you to stay true to your values, especially when you encounter adversity. A deeper understanding and awareness of ourselves also helps us make more informed decisions about our future goals and how to move forward.

The bottom line is that it is very important for you to take time to get to know yourself. Building your self-awareness can be fostered through a variety of activities, from a simple personality test to an ongoing meditation and mindfulness practice. Other activities include being reflective, spending time in a connected relationship that provides reflection and feedback, and asking questions. Some of the questions to consider include:

- How do you like to connect with your friends and family, or use your free time?
- What is something you are interested in learning more about?
- Who influences or inspires you?
- What brings you a sense of gratitude?
- When did you last feel proud of yourself?

Paying attention to ourselves to develop a greater sense of self-awareness helps us navigate not only the external world, but the internal one as well. If we are unaware of how we feel when we are in a particular state of being, it becomes more challenging to properly respond in order to get the very things we need to thrive and to meet the needs of those around us.

Reflective practices help build self-awareness, especially when it is a continual practice of inquiry. Engaging in a regular practice of reflection, and perhaps even a dialogue about this practice with loved ones and/or colleagues, benefits everyone. Through a reflective practice you begin to know what pushes your buttons or brings you great joy. When we share our stories, whether stories of success or failure, we express our frustrations and celebrations, our words of wisdom, and our cries for help. We also create the opportunity for others to share their stories. If we really listen and pay attention, we increase our awareness and understanding of ourself and others. Raising our consciousness to these reflective practices prevents us from falling into a cycle of immediately reacting to our thoughts and emotions.

Our oversaturated, fast-paced days that offer very little down-time, make it very challenging to truly gain an awareness of ourselves or those around us. With greater self-awareness comes the ability to practice empathy and serve as a stronger advocate. So, examine yourself with courage, truth, grace, and love to get to know yourself a little bit better.

Increasing Your Self-Awareness

Write down your response to the following questions to increase your self-awareness:

Are you eager to get up and go to work, or more often than not, eager for time away from work?

_____

When you speak about your work, is it often as a complaint or with criticism, or is it with contentment?

_____

Do you feel like your work reflects what you value?

_____

Are you confident in yourself and the work you are doing?

_____

Do you have a clear sense of purpose?

_____

Are you able to focus on the present, or does your mind often feel somewhere else?

_____

Do you feel connected and supported by those you work with?

_____

Can you speak honestly about how you are doing?

_____

Do you transition from one thing to another with ease or with a sense of urgency?

_____

When you receive feedback, can you still recognize your strengths?

_____

Can you reflect on how you are doing and adjust accordingly without guilt or shame?

_____

Do you have healthy ways to cope when you are feeling sad, or lonely, etc. (fill in the blank with a variety of emotions)?

_____

Are the people important to you aware that you care for them, even as you care for yourself?

_____

CHAPTER 27

WHAT EXACTLY IS SELF-CARE?

Self-care can simply be defined as taking care of yourself, but it's a little more complicated than that.

Similar to myself and others, you may think that by practicing self-care, you are being selfish. It is hard to believe that anyone in their right mind would intentionally be selfish, so it can't be a practice that a considerate and loving individual would be willing to do, right? But when we constantly try to achieve the unachievable, we begin to feel worn down and exhausted, and when we feel and function in this way, we can do little more than simply survive. Self-care helps us avoid this scenario.

There are multiple ways in which we take care of ourselves. I'm sure you are familiar with Maslow's hierarchy of needs and how our needs build upon one another. Unless we can meet our needs at the most basic level, it is unlikely that we will be successful in meeting our higher-level needs. In her book *Take Time for You,* Tina Boogren invites readers to explore the frequency in which they meet their needs as related to physiology, safety, belonging, esteem, self-actualization, and transcendence. As an individual, you may find that you are doing well in one aspect, but need a lot more support in another.

There is no blueprint or one-size-fits all method that I can offer you that will allow you to quickly check this off your to-do list. This is a journey of self-exploration that leads you closer to a meaningful and more effective practice of self-care. Self-care comes through positive action that occurs on a consistent basis. It is a process that includes growth, challenges, setbacks, and rewards. These consistent practices help us embark on the journey of self-discovery to build our self-awareness and promote well-being. Traveling down this road will help you build your capacity to practice resilience. Much like professional development experiences, the more we put in, the more we get out. Basically, if you don't use it, you lose it.

The only thing we can count on in life is change. Think about the early days of the COVID-19 pandemic. It seemed as if daily things were shifting and changing. Is it possible that this global pandemic will be the impetus for us to care for ourselves and, ultimately, the greater community? According to *The Resilient Practitioner*, there can be a tension between "other-care and self-care" but, for those of us in caregiver positions like educating, self-care is a sacred obligation. Is it possible that the practice of self-care could actually lead to community care, then to greater transformation and systemic change? Let's advocate to foster well-being and build resilience to help create more healthy educational communities.

True self-care is knowing who you are and how you are.

Your journey toward a healthier state of well-being begins with the practice of intention setting. What do you truly want to be, and how do you want to move forward? This is where you can begin to build your plan in a way that creates sustainability and helps you feel more supported and cared for by yourself and others. Then, when you are ready, choose one thing that moves you toward improving your well-being. After that, choose three things that will move you even further toward your goal of enhancing your well-being. Remember, this journey is not a one-and-done practice, but more of a daily ritual to keep moving in a direction that promotes care and repair and builds resilience.

Now, breathe deep. You are smart and capable. You have so much to offer. You are strong and wise. You can do this hard work. Remember to keep coming back to yourself again and again, because you matter.

SELF-CARE IS ABOUT KNOWING **WHO** YOU ARE AND **HOW** YOU ARE

Practicing Self-Care

What intention do you want to set for yourself regarding a practice of self-care? What are some of the things you do to take care of your body, mind, and spirit? What is one thing you would like to start doing more of?

_____

_____

_____

_____

_____

_____

_____

_____

_____

_____

_____

_____

_____

_____

CHAPTER 28

CONNECTING THE MIND AND THE BODY

"If you can settle your body, you are more likely to be calm, alert, and fully present, no matter what is going on around you.... A calm, settled body is the foundation for health, for healing, for helping others, and for changing the world."

—Resmaa Menakem, author of *My Grandmother's Hands: Racialized Trauma and the Pathway to Mending Our Hearts and Bodies*

The mind and body are intricately connected. To care for one allows us to better care for the other. We often live disconnected from others, and even more unfortunately, from ourselves. We may move through the day with our bodies in one place and our minds in another.

When we pause to increase our awareness, we invite ourselves to settle in and experience the connectedness between mind and body. This allows us to recalibrate and decide how we want to move forward, rather than just react to any given moment. In this pause, we are also given the opportunity to accept, appreciate, and nurture our body.

In *Sitting Still Like a Frog*, Eline Snel shares that children, much like adults, "have a tendency to just keep going. By regularly pressing the pause button, you give yourself the time and space to notice that you are breathing and to feel what is going on inside of you. And as soon as you notice, you have a choice: shall I continue with what I was doing, or do I need a short break, or do I need something else?"[36]

It wasn't until I participated in trauma-informed yoga training that I became aware of the strong connection between the breath and the body. Within our body is the autonomic nervous system. The autonomic nervous system is subdivided into the sympathetic nervous system and the parasympathetic nervous system. Each of these systems play a significant but distinct role in how they impact and control our bodies. Simply speaking, the sympathetic nervous system aids in quick responses that accelerate our heart rate and promote fight-or-flight behaviors. In essence, the sympathetic nervous system helps us survive. When this system is "in charge," our prefrontal cortex goes offline and automatic processes take over. However, experiencing too much of this puts us on the road to burnout. The parasympathetic nervous system, on the other hand, aids in slowing things down to promote rest and digestion. Simply put, it helps us recover. It now makes sense why it is critically important for us to experience some form of quality rest in order to maintain our health, doesn't it?

Stephen Porges, professor of psychiatry and founding director of the Traumatic Stress Research Consortium, is well known for his work surrounding the polyvagal theory, an explanation for how we experience safety, connection, or fight/flight behaviors, and the vagus nerve, which is connected to the parasympathetic nervous system. According to Porges, the strength of an individual's vagal tone is directly connected to their parasympathetic nervous system and their ability to respond in a more calming manner to changes, stress, and pressure.[37] Porges' theory has led to multiple studies, and as Jena Pincott states in her book, *Wits, Guts, Grit,* anything that's linked to resilience touches on the vagus nerve. Examples include gut microbiomes, nature, exercise, affectionate touch, and more. "If there is a key to self-regulation, resilience, and health, it involves a well-strummed vagus nerve."[38]

CHAPTER 29

FOSTERING THE "MUSCLES OF RESILIENCE"

Our ability to pause, notice, pay attention, and move our bodies helps us strengthen our vagus nerve and our capacity for resilience. Strengthening our "muscles of resilience" can occur in a variety of ways. Some of these practices can be accessed immediately and take no more than five minutes, while others require more time and planning.

- *Get moving.* I know, I know, it can be so hard to fit in a workout, especially when there is so much else to do. However, exercise, particularly consistent exercise, can improve an individual's heart rate. In addition, yoga activates the parasympathetic nervous system and improves overall mental and physical health.

- *Sing.* Humming and singing, particularly in unison with others, increases heart rate variability and activates the vagus nerve in the back of the throat.

- *Let out a laugh.* Some say laughter is the best medicine. It certainly has its health benefits. Laughter impacts the heart rate, stimulates the vagus nerve, and activates the parasympathetic nervous system. Humor helps to carry us through even the most challenging moments.

- *Get outside.* Nature offers some breathtaking opportunities to reset. If you can, enjoy your lunch outdoors. If you can't get outside, bring the outdoors in by adding some fresh flowers or plants to your workspace.

- *Consider what you eat.* As they say, you are what you eat. Certain foods help us feel healthier. We often feel like we don't have the time or energy to prepare a nutritious meal. But your gut health is actually connected to your vagus nerve and increasing the amount of bifidobacterium (gut bugs) in your system has a soothing effect on the nervous system. So, drink your kombucha and take your probiotics!

- *Rest and relax.* Find ways to relax and rest, even if that means you must set some boundaries and restrict the times you pick up the phone, check email, etc. Relaxing allows us to experience a sense of calm and clarity. You have permission to pause. Whether you choose to relax by taking a bath, drinking a cup of tea, or practicing yoga or meditation, relaxing slows down your heart rate and reduces blood pressure and tension. Rest, though different from relaxation, is just as important. Our bodies need sleep to feel restored. It is important to try to get seven or eight hours of sleep each night. To achieve that goal, consider setting an alarm to go off 30 minutes before you want to go to bed. When the alarm goes off, no matter what you are doing, begin the process of getting ready for bed.

A Personal Account of Building Resilience

—Tami W., 3rd-grade teacher

When I reflect back on why I went into education, it isn't one of those stories that you hear and tear up over because it is just so beautiful, special, or moving. I recognize that I didn't have that cloud-parting moment when my vision cleared to declare "I'm going to be a teacher." It was just always what I felt like I would do. My dad was an elementary teacher and my grandfather was a secondary teacher and principal. I liked the idea of teaching, and my parents would always tell me, "You should think about becoming a teacher when you grow up." I know. It's not very glamorous, right? However, I have always been a driven person, especially in regard to helping others. So, the idea of teaching made sense to me, and it felt right. I knew I could help kids and work with them to help them grow and learn. Little did I know, back when I started the teaching program at my local university, just how much this job would challenge and overwhelm me.

When I began my teaching career, I knew that this profession was going to be a difficult job from talking with some of my mentors who were teachers themselves. However, nothing quite prepares you for your first year of teaching. At the age of 25, I was the most exhausted I had ever been. During this time, I also started to recognize that something wasn't quite right with my health. Despite the terrible pain I was in, I felt there was no choice but to push through and keep marching on because kids depended on me, and I could not and would not let them down. Even with frequent setbacks of stomach pain, headaches, and aching joints that prevented me from sitting much at all because of the pain I experienced when trying to stand back up again, I kept marching on. The exhaustion persisted throughout my first year of teaching. I'll be honest, I never sought help for my symptoms during my first year, because taking care of myself was not on my agenda. I had papers to grade, lessons to prepare, and kids to teach. I was trying to do my job well. I didn't have time for me, or at least that is what I would tell myself.

Unfortunately, my health did not improve and during my second year of teaching, I finally realized that something needed to change. It came to the point where my joints hurt so badly after sitting in any position, or even from sleeping, that I would have to take several minutes every morning to slowly move from a position of lying down to standing up. It wasn't until spring break when I felt that I had time to finally see someone to try to figure out what to do about my health. During this time, I found out that I had food sensitivities that were playing a big role in my chronic pain. While I was relieved to find out that I could start feeling better and have increased energy to bring to my job, I was also very disappointed to give up many of my favorite foods. Plus, this meant no more quick, easy, convenience foods. Now my husband and I would actually have to take the time to cook. This stressed me out because I knew how little time I already had since I was always overwhelmed by school, deadlines, and well, everything.

Finding out that you can't eat certain foods can actually change your life in a positive way. After understanding what foods made me feel better, I began researching recipes that would make eating fun again. This is when I finally realized that if I did not prioritize my health, and if I kept on the initial path from when I first started teaching, it would not be sustainable. I did not take time for myself or even think about what made me feel healthy or happy. Instead, I went through my day focusing on getting it all done and moving on to the next to-do item. Once I slowed down, prioritized my health, and planned out meals in order to experience less pain, I realized that I actually loved cooking. It became my new passion and brought me joy. I would listen to music and cook new recipes, and it felt amazing! Not only was I healing physically from removing foods that did not serve me, but my mindset began to shift as well.

I will soon be entering my eleventh year of teaching. It's surreal to think back to the beginning years of my teaching career and recall how hard I was working to try and stay afloat. Teaching is difficult work. I still get overwhelmed by all of the tasks that need to get done and could easily come up with reasons that I can't make the time to take care of myself. However, I also understand that I need to prioritize my well-being to be the teacher that I want to be, not just for my students, but for myself.

A Creative Reset, by Kay Waterson

For many people, creative art can be a fun hobby, an exciting area of study, or a rewarding career. Whatever your relationship with the arts might be, we all benefit from learning about the cognitive impact that creative art processes have on the healing of trauma and the management of stress.

In recent years, art and craft activities have been recognized as a trendy and joyful self-care strategy. Embroidery, adult coloring books, and DIY furniture or home projects are just a few examples of different popular activities.

When you participate in creative art activities and thought processes, you are also engaging in a process that has been shown to yield positive cognitive and emotional results. A recent study conducted by Drexel University found that a 45-minute session of art making can significantly lower the body's stress hormone cortisol levels.[39] Participants in this study were diverse in terms of age, gender, race, and personal histories. Many adults are hesitant to pick up a paintbrush, but remember, it is not about the quality of the product you produce. You are, in fact, neurologically benefiting from the process of engaging with your materials! As educators, we know that our ideal learning state takes place just outside of our comfort zone of proximal development. I encourage you to carve out some time for an old or new hobby when you are in need of some stress reduction.

Remember, creative activity can alleviate symptoms of chronic stress and vicarious trauma, such as depression and severe anxiety. It is a powerful, and sometimes overlooked, strategy for managing stress and engaging in introspective thought.

Choosing this strategy for your own self-care can help you feel refreshed and lower your cortisol levels. Choosing to engage in art activities with your students can also be a joyful and rewarding experience. Students are interested in learning about the brain, too, so be sure to share with them some basic psychological concepts about why creating art feels so great!

Engaging in Creative Art Activities

Here are some creative art activities that you can do at home to build resiliency and lower stress levels:

- Origami
- Calligraphy
- Draw with dry mediums like colored pencils, charcoal, pastels, or graphite
- Paint with wet mediums like ink, acrylic or oil paint, watercolor, or dye
- Sculpt with clay or playdough
- Shape, bend, or manipulate wire into a three-dimensional design
- Sew, braid, or make jewelry
- Engage in woodworking, carving, or whittling
- Spray-paint old knick-knacks or natural materials such as sticks or pinecones
- Create classroom posters or worksheets using free graphic design apps like Canva
- Knit, embroider, or weave
- Take pictures or play with photography filters and editing features on your phone
- Learn about a new subject using online tutorials
- Redesign a room in your house
- Write a letter to a loved one using only pictures
- Create a mandala using natural materials
- Arrange flowers or plants
- Create a bonsai or zen garden
- Repurpose old magazines and create a collage
- Illustrate your favorite quotes using colorful markers
- Work with tiles to create a mosaic piece or a home improvement project
- Go outside and get creative with sidewalk chalk

Spend a few minutes thinking about which of these activities appeal to you. Highlight those with a marker for future reference.

If you aren't sure where to start, feel free to grab some colored pencils or markers and start coloring the image on the following page!

DON'T JUST SURVIVE. **THRIVE**

CHAPTER 30

DON'T FORGET TO BREATHE

"Breathe! You are alive!"

—Thich Nhat Hanh

I am hoping we've all had the pleasure of studying some form of life cycles. My personal favorite was always the life cycle of a butterfly. More broadly speaking, cycles emphasize movement and the opportunity to return to an experience. What I love about cycles is that they remind us that so much of life is an ongoing process, happening over a period of time and experienced again and again. Focusing on the broader concept of a cycle personally gives me hope that very rarely does something remain stuck forever.

Breath regulation affects our emotional regulation, which ultimately affects our clarity and thinking. The way we feel changes how we breathe and the way we breathe changes how we feel.

Having conscious awareness of breathing, or mindful breathing, can shift our nervous system, unite our bodies with our minds, and help put us back in the present moment. The beauty of any type of breath practice is that you can begin at any time and it can essentially be practiced anywhere. When we begin to breathe with awareness and intention, specifically when we can lengthen our exhale, we help our body shift into that parasympathetic state of rest and digest. So, shall we invite a little awareness to the breath?

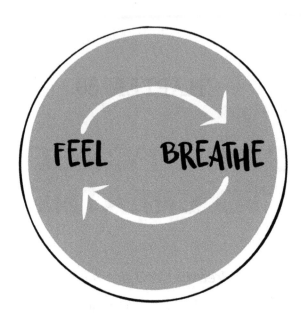

- Start by focusing on your breath, bringing awareness to the sensation of each inhale and exhale.

- Chances are your mind will wander, and that is okay. Simply bring yourself back to the present moment by focusing once again on your inhale and exhale.

- See if you can take three rounds of breath to the count of three, inhaling and exhaling as a complete cycle, before you move on with your day. When this comes with ease, begin to increase the length of time or the rounds of breath you take with awareness.

- In moments when you are feeling particularly strong emotions, try to breathe in through your nose and out through your mouth.

- Practice mindful breathing anywhere, while you are preparing for your day, waiting at a stoplight, standing in line, using the copier, or warming up your cold cup of coffee or lunch. You really can practice it anywhere.

- At times you may want to consider pairing your inhale and exhale with a phrase or affirmation. Some examples of this include:

- Inhale—Peace, Exhale—Calm

- Inhale—Gratitude, Exhale—Love

- Inhale—"Help me," Exhale—"Love well," "Teach well," "Be well"

- Inhale—"I can receive ___ (love, help)," Exhale—I can release _____ (fear, worry)"

- Inhale—Right here, Exhale—Right now

Quite honestly, you can use whatever word or phrase feels appropriate and comforting to you at the moment, which is why I appreciate this practice so much. It becomes a very simple way to offer myself some comfort and compassion.

Another type of supportive breathing exercise is called the box breath. Box breathing is a simple, yet effective technique that can be used anytime you experience stress or anxiety. It is a breathing practice that athletes, members of the military, and first responders often use because it is so effective in releasing stress and regulating the autonomic nervous system so you can experience a clear mind, improved focus, and relaxation. It also helps lower your blood pressure and heart rate, while increasing energy and blood flow to the heart and lungs.

So, what exactly is the box breath? Well, to begin, and in order to experience the full range of benefits, you want to ensure that you are breathing all the way into the belly, otherwise known as diaphragmatic breathing. If you are unsure how to breathe into your belly, spend some time lying on your back with one hand resting on your belly, noticing how the belly rises and falls with each breath cycle. Once you feel confident in what this feels like within your body, you can practice box breathing either lying down, sitting up, or even standing. Here is a guide to box breath:

❑ Begin by breathing in and out through your nose.

❑ Inhale through the nose for four seconds, allowing your breath to fill up your belly like a balloon.

❑ Pause the breath for four seconds.

❑ Exhale through the nose for four seconds.

❏ Pause the breath for four seconds.

❏ Repeat this cycle three to five times.

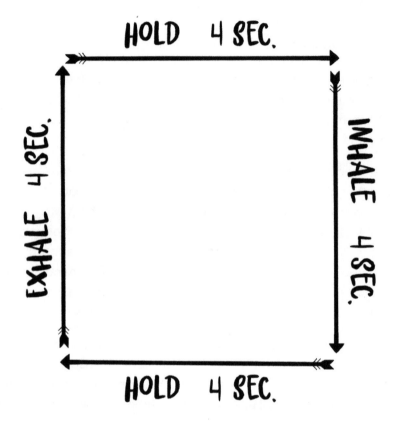

DON'T JUST SURVIVE. **THRIVE**

A Personal Account of Building Resilience

—Annie F., educator and cofounder of Blue Bridge School

I backed into teaching almost by accident. The summer after I graduated from college, I was working in the refrigerated room of a grocery store packing precooked food. It was August in New Orleans. I would walk to work in the extreme heat and humidity. Upon arrival, I'd layer up as if I was walking out into a Chicago snowstorm. On one of those long chilly days in the fridge, I was enjoying an al fresco lunch break alone to thaw out when I happened upon a "Teacher Wanted" ad in the newspaper.

Teaching had often been in the back of my mind as a career option, but always as a backup. I loved the idea of teaching, but I went to college to study photojournalism. I wanted an exotic life full of travel. I had many phenomenal teachers in my extended family, even my parents were teachers when they first met. They were all wonderful people, but they were also just so settled. When I was 18 and hoping to shake things up in this world, I wondered if I could be a powerhouse feminist, smashing the patriarchy as a schoolteacher. I had three older sisters who were dominating in business roles. Could I really change the world through teaching?

Ironic, right? What job has more world-changing superpowers than teaching?

Later that August, I accepted the position from the newspaper ad to teach Spanish at a kindergarten through 8th grade Catholic school serving mostly white, fairly privileged kids. I was filling in the position for someone who had gone out in flames, so the expectations were low. I was 22 and a job with low expectations was a good match for me.

As a new teacher, single with no family, I had time on my hands, so I found an afterschool gig. I taught Spanish to a pre-kindergarten group in a New Orleans public school aftercare program. I worked with the kids on the carpet while the lead teacher, Ms. T, helped students finish schoolwork. Or at least that's what I thought was happening. I never really knew where I was going or what I was doing there. My general strategy was to be quiet and not ask too many questions. I was a very fresh educator, and that showed. If the kids got rowdy, Ms. T. would threaten to get her stick. If I didn't show up, the kids would watch fuzzy cartoons on PBS.

On the surface, the disparities between these two school settings were wildly apparent. Upon closer look, I realized as different as these schools were, the students faced a similar set of challenges. In both settings, children had adults holding them to high levels of expectation of self-regulation and control without offering much support on how to achieve this. I saw children in both institutions attempting to process major life events, trauma, and real stress.

It was the early 2000s and much of the educational system was focused on standardizing academic benchmarks. There wasn't an emphasis on the touchy-feely side of education. There wasn't space in the day to teach self-regulation and control. In both settings, it seemed that by kindergarten, a child could easily have a lifelong label for what kind of student they were.

Since college, I had relied heavily on yoga and mindfulness for my own self-maintenance. Out of the need for classroom crowd control, I employed elements of those practices with my students from day one. My first year teaching I had a group of particularly boisterous 5th graders right in the middle of the day. At noon every day, church bells rang just outside my classroom window. Instead of shouting over the combination of bells and preteen energy, together we took that minute to breathe in silence. Yes, there were giggles but as it became routine, there were fewer giggly outbursts. The church bells would stop ringing, and our class would start up again, but always with a totally different energy level.

After those early years teaching in New Orleans, I did use my career as a means for exploration, travel, and self-discovery. After a handful of moves around the world, I found myself in the mountains of Wyoming. There I found my passion within education lies in the early childhood years. I love watching the brain development from birth through the early years of school. I especially love working with families and children in their first five years of life. I enjoyed a brief stint as a teacher in a toddler room before moving into an administrative role.

DON'T JUST SURVIVE, **THRIVE**

In preschool, turnover is high among both faculty and students. Children are expelled at rates higher than at any other educational level. While there are a number of compounding factors, the story plays out similarly most times. Educators are under-resourced to respond appropriately to chronic challenging behavior. Something has to give, either the child or the teacher. As the director of a non-profit child care program in 2011, this suddenly became my problem to solve.

Just as I noticed with my students in those early years, I saw a mismatch between what was being asked of teachers and a lack of support for proper implementation. Teachers needed skills to prevent, recognize, and respond to challenging behavior. They needed support as they processed these challenging and often traumatic classroom experiences.

Self-care was a buzzword growing in popularity at the time. Our team of teachers and administrators collectively came to realize that self-care doesn't work without community care first. Neither teachers nor students could achieve what was being asked of them without support from those around them. As a faculty, we developed new skills and put them into practice. We created a system of community care. It wasn't a perfect system. There was almost constant reevaluation. The best systems are agile to allow change for new people, new group dynamics, new needs, etc. Taking care of our village required an ongoing commitment. Teachers, administrators, families, all the stakeholders were involved in this community care to tend to the village wellness.

Finding a moment to be quiet and breathe was our starting point. This breath work can be done in almost any setting, as a group or as an individual. Children or adults can use it. It is adaptable. It can be as short as taking one conscious breath in a stressful meeting or when behavior needs a near-immediate intervention. In non-crisis moments, a round of three to five breaths can reset the energy of a group. With very young children or a group new to each other, it can be introduced in a playful way. Finding moments of pause is a collaborative experience, an offering, not a forced moment of time out.

One way to take this practice deeper is to link the breath with a brief body scan. I have found nearly any group, kids or adults, can tolerate three breaths. Here is a sample offering:

Inhale, scan your body from the ground up. Identify where you are connected to the earth.

Exhale, allow yourself to feel supported by the surface holding you.

Inhale, notice where you are holding tension or feeling sensation in your body.

Exhale, expand, release and find more space inside your body.

Inhale, tune into your brain and any sensations you're noticing there; notice where your thoughts are.

Exhale, allow those sensations and thoughts to settle.

Through routine practice, participants can learn how to tap into their breath in order to access a moment of reset. Breath is portable. Breath is accessible to all who are living. Through regular practice with teachers, families, and adults, a practice of community care is built. A culture of village wellness is established.

Now I find myself in Michigan about to embark on a new professional journey in early childhood. Through all of this work and these collected experiences, I have come to realize the incredible value of those noontime New Orleans church bells. That daily moment gave our class a built-in pause. That pause turned into a lasting practice for community care.

CHAPTER 31

THE INVITATION TO BE MORE MINDFUL

"A mindfulness practice can shape how we are in the world: our view, our core values, and our deep sense of purpose and meaning."

—Thich Nhat Hanh

Mindfulness is defined as purposely paying attention to a particular thing. Whether that is your breath, the sounds you hear, or the act of eating, the goal is to become completely aware of the present moment. Mindfulness is a vital component to our health, well-being, and resilience. In order for students to learn, we must activate their curiosity and get them to pay attention and focus on the information presented. Children are naturally inquisitive and curious, so being present in the moment comes naturally to them. Adults need to do the same to practice mindfulness.

There are a multitude of resources available to help us integrate social emotional learning and mindfulness practices into the classroom. As adults, we also need to learn to integrate these practices into our daily lives.

When I first started meditating and practicing mindfulness, it was typically first thing in the morning. While this is a great way to start each day, I realized that I wanted more of these moments throughout the day. I began to try and find ways to incorporate moments of mindfulness into various points of my day, especially when I felt stressed. It didn't take me long to find endless opportunities for such moments.

Transitions from one part of the day to another are a great way to welcome in more awareness and presence. We go through a number of transitions over the course of our day. Think of each transition as an opportunity to pause, check in, and recalibrate. Since we can't add more minutes to the day, how can we use our daily transitions from home to work, while at work, and from work to home, to summon in more awareness?

Moving Mindfully

... As You Begin the Day

- Stretch and allow yourself to take three full deep belly breaths before climbing out of bed in the morning.

- Listen to the sound of the water, feel the temperature of the water, notice the feel of the water as it washes over you, and smell your soap or shampoo in your daily shower.

- Focus on the smell and taste of your toothpaste and the physical sensations you experience while brushing your teeth.

- Pay attention to the taste, the smell, and the temperature of your food while eating your breakfast. Savor each bite or sip, taking in as much as you can.

- Take three deep belly breaths when you get into your vehicle to drive to work.

- Take a brief walk around the school building before jumping in to the work day. Pay attention to the colors and sounds that surround you.

... Through the Building

- Inhale and exhale before you resume your normal pace and before you move forward when opening or stepping through a doorway.

- Notice the colors, temperature, sound, and smells when you enter your classroom.

- Focus on a wall hanging and take a deep breath as you notice the colors, shapes, and texture of this particular object while you wait for your computer to turn on.

- Stop what you are doing and take one full deep belly breath when you hear the sound of the school bell.

- Stretch your body and notice any points of sensation or tension before you leave the teachers' lounge.

- Massage each finger and focus on the temperature of the water when you wash your hands.

- Pause at the doorway, breathe, and tune in to your emotions when you leave your classroom. As you acknowledge these feelings, is there anything you would like to offer yourself before transitioning home?
- Offer yourself a positive affirmation or a long exhale to release any stress you may have felt during the day before you leave school.
- Try to get in three rounds of deep breathing while waiting in traffic or at a stop light before the vehicle needs to move forward again.
- Take a full deep breath before your evening meal and then focus on the taste, smell, and texture of your food.
- Recall one good thing that happened in your day and then note the emotions and sensations you are experiencing before you turn off the light to go to bed.

In no way am I expecting you to do every one of these suggestions, but begin by choosing one to become a consistent practice. Then consider adding one or two more practices of mindfulness into your daily transitions.

Practice Mindfulness
During Recess Duty

Ways to Practice Mindfulness During Extra Duty

Many of you have extra duty responsibilities throughout the week, such as in the lunchroom, at arrival or dismissal, or during recess or an art, movement, media, or music activity. Think of ways to sneak in a few moments to pause, become aware, and reconnect to yourself and what is going on around you while performing these responsibilities.

At one point during my career, I had at least one daily recess duty assignment. Recess was a particularly stressful time. Kids were often running around and screaming and yelling. On occasion there were incidents of physical aggression during recess. I found myself dreading my time outside on the playground and wishing that something would change. One day I noticed a student crouched down near the base of a sycamore tree. He was collecting vibrant red leaves that had fallen from the tree, and he continued to do this over the next few days. I viewed this as an invitation for a change. As I got into the routine of walking over to the sycamore tree each time I stepped outside, I eventually paired it with a brief pause. This pause allowed me to place my back against that tall tree trunk, sink in and feel its support, draw in a deep breath or two, and then move from there.

Here are a few ways to add in more awareness during extra duty:

- Notice the texture of each clothing item and each point of contact against your skin as you put on layers of clothing to head outside for recess duty.
- Use the doorway to exit the building as an opportunity to pause and take a deep breath.
- Identify a location such as a bench, a tree, or a grassy field, and then make contact with it by placing your back against the object each time you go outside for duty.
- Take three deep breaths.
- Look around and notice the sky, the landscape, and the colors you see.
- Listen to the sounds you hear and note the emotions you feel.

- Notice if there is any tension in your body and if you can find a way to release that tension.

After you have established a consistent routine for practicing mindfulness during your extra duty, you can begin to pay attention to other things. For example, pay attention to all of the acts of kindness you observe from students and staff. On another day, take note of all the moments that bring joy and laughter to yourself or others. On another day, pay attention to all of the colors you see. What else could you focus on during these moments?

Loving Kindness

"Hate cannot drive out hate; only love can do that."

—Martin Luther King, Jr.

Loving kindness practices always start with focusing on your individual self. This is where we must begin in order to have a real impact in our communities and the world as a whole. Kristin Neff's research on self-compassion examines how our ability to have compassion for others is connected to our capacity to understand our own humanity and have compassion for ourselves as well.[40] When we recognize our self-worth, we are more likely to recognize the worth of others, and respond with less judgement and more kindness.

We all encounter experiences that create anger, resentment, guilt, and more. These negative emotions can become stumbling blocks to forgiving and offering compassion to ourselves and others. When we practice loving kindness we experience less self-criticism and self-destructive thoughts, a reduction in pain symptoms, more positive emotions, faster recoveries, and increased resilience.[41] In the practice of loving kindness, we strive to offer love, empathy, kindness, and understanding. It begins with ourselves and then spills over toward others.

> "You yourself, as much as anybody in the entire universe, deserve your love and affection."
>
> —Sharon Salzberg

Loving Kindness Meditation for Educators

This meditation aids in developing friendly, kind, and loving thoughts toward ourselves and then ripples out into the world toward others.

- Sit in a comfortable seat.
- Bring length to your spine without being rigid. Allow your shoulders to relax and then rest your hands in your lap or gently on your knees.
- Close your eyes.
- Release tension around your lips, your jaw, and your forehead.
- Relax and settle in but remain alert.
- Notice your breathing as it moves in and out of the body.
- Inhale deeply, feel your ribs expand and then soften as you exhale, and then release the breath out of the body.
- Place your hands over your heart as you silently repeat the following words to yourself:
  - May I be happy
  - May I be well
  - May I be safe
  - May I be at peace
- Repeat these words again, savoring each phrase as you say it.

- Think of a student. Holding that student in mind, extend these same phrases to them:
  - May you be happy
  - May you be well
  - May you be safe
  - May you be at peace
- Think of a colleague that you interact with at work. Holding this individual in mind, extend these phrases to them:
  - May you be happy
  - May you be well
  - May you be safe
  - May you be at peace
- Sit in this kind, loving space you've created for yourself and for others.
- Take a nice deep breath in and as you exhale, bring yourself back to your surroundings.
- Be kind and patient with yourself as you develop this practice.

Remember, when we treat ourselves with loving kindness, our personal well-being increases and we become more capable of caring for those around us with more ease and tenderness. Taking care of others becomes easier and far more enriching and nourishing when we take care of who we are first.

CHAPTER 32

THE MESSAGES WE SURROUND OURSELVES WITH COUNT

"Always remember you are braver than you believe, stronger than you seem, smarter than you think, and loved more than you know."

—A. A. Milne

My second year of teaching, I moved into a position teaching the overflow students from 1st grade. The principal informed me that I would be teaching the "cast-off" students with challenging behaviors. Encouraging, right? I was determined to remain positive and hopeful. I met with the other kindergarten teachers to learn more about my future students. I started hearing stories that alluded to the challenges created by these students. The stories made me more and more concerned. I was warned about one student in particular over and over again.

As the first day neared, my excitement and nervousness grew. I spent a lot of time wondering if I was capable of leading these children. Finally, the big day arrived and with it, so did the students, except for the one that I had been warned about. Maybe, I thought, I got lucky and he isn't attending this school anymore. I remember releasing my shoulders and breathing a little deeper. As I made it through the first morning, my optimism grew. Perhaps this would indeed be a good year with a great group of students!

After picking up the students from lunch, we returned to the classroom and settled into the carpeted area to read a story together. Then we heard a knock on the door. I opened it to find a parent and child standing outside my door. I knelt down and held out my hand to meet and welcome in the student. Instead of greeting me with a smile or even returning my handshake, he looked me straight in the eye, dragged a finger across his neck, and spoke with pure confidence, "I'm going to slit your f***ing throat and let you bleed to death." I was shocked and thought to myself, "Well alright then, best make sure I don't leave any knives laying around." And on that note, I stood up and held the door open as I said, "Welcome to 1st grade!"

I received no training during my five years of preservice education that prepared me for this situation. I thought having a student masturbate during a small group reading lesson would be the most unpredictable and uncomfortable encounter of my career. Little did I know! As you can imagine, things didn't stop there and the student's "bad" behavior escalated more and more throughout the coming days and weeks. I took copious notes documenting every observable behavior. I encountered situations that I never imagined. I was at a complete loss. What in the world was I supposed to do? Fortunately, I didn't work alone. I sought out my principal, the instructional facilitator, and several of the special education teachers throughout the district. Unfortunately, no one else really knew what to do because their education had not prepared them for anything like this, either. We would often stare at each other with puzzled looks or blank faces.

After a particularly challenging day that left me feeling defeated, overwhelmed, and heartbroken, one of the special education teachers walked into my classroom and placed a sticker of a royal blue tang fish on my shirt. All she said was, "Just keep swimming," and then she turned and left my room.

"What in the world?" I thought. "Is she being serious right now? How is this supposed to help me?!" But this silly little phrase did start to help me. Eventually, it served as a reminder to just keep moving forward. On the days that felt especially challenging, I would pull out a sheet of those same stickers and give one to each of my students to place on their shirt. They were ecstatic to receive a sticker, and I was grateful for the 15 visual reminders of this message staring me in the face. It helped me remember that whatever happened, go with the flow and stop resisting so much. It gave me a sense of hope. It reminded me to breathe, and then breathe again. We've had hard days before and we will have hard days again, but we will get through them. This message kept me afloat throughout the year. It didn't demand that I get it all right or find all of the answers to the problems that needed to be solved. It simply reminded me to keep going. Who knew that the perseverance I found in my second year of teaching would come from a sticker?

The messages we surround ourselves with make a difference, whether we are aware of it or not. They may even become the mantra that keeps us going in even the most difficult of times.

This quote by A. A. Milne hangs on the wall of my daughter's bedroom: "Always remember you are braver than you believe, stronger than you seem, smarter than you think, and loved more than you know." It was a piece of art I created while anxiously awaiting her arrival. I read those words over and over, offering them often as a prayer, with the hope that one day she would know them to be true. Despite them hanging up on her wall, I don't think I spoke them aloud to her consistently. Then one day, I told her, "You know little lady, you are smarter than you think." Without skipping a beat, she replied, "and loved more than you know." Suddenly, I was reminded once again about the significance of the messages we surround ourselves with. Surround yourself with words that inspire you, and keep you going. Then, start spreading those messages to those around you.

Messages of Hope and Inspiration

Jot down a few hopeful and inspirational messages to surround yourself with in your home and in the workplace. What kind of impact do you think they will have on any given situation?

_____

_____

_____

_____

_____

| You can do hard things! | Breathe deep. | | |
| I see your hard work! | Keep going, you are changing lives! | | |

CHAPTER 33

THE MESSAGES WE TELL OURSELVES MATTER

Validation. Acceptance. Affirmation. Approval. We all long to experience these feelings. For many of us, when things were abruptly disrupted from the pandemic, the validation and feedback we received from our students and colleagues were suddenly cut off. So, who did we turn to for validation? Most of us turned to an internal dialogue. When our only source of feedback is internal, it becomes imperative to consider the stories we tell ourselves.

Most of us have a negative bias against ourselves. We are conditioned to look for deficits or weaknesses and make improvements. Remember though, failure is part of success, and the important thing is to try again, and again. Growth and improvement are how we measure success, right?

It is crucial to understand that self-dialogue is tied to an individual's neurological structures. Professionals who encounter frequent exposure to toxic stress or vicarious trauma often form habits of self-deprecating inner dialogue. Paying attention to the tone of our self-dialogue can help us notice spikes in states of arousal. When we think to ourselves "I am not enough," we are operating in a state of hyperarousal. To maintain healthy self-care practices, it is important to ask, "Am I speaking gently with myself?" or "What are my regulatory needs?"

The stories we tell ourselves matter, so speak kindly to yourself. Words have power. When we connect affirmations, internal dialogue, and mindset, we impact the way in which we interact with students and colleagues, and even how we view the work we do. When we speak harshly, we tend to respond harshly. When we speak with kindness, we respond with kindness.

> # What you focus on grows.

We are all going to make mistakes, fall short, and feel like a failure at times. Tamara Levitt, head of content of the meditation app Calm once said, "Just because you have a failure, it does not mean that you are a failure. So, fail proudly, gently, beautifully." Instead of focusing on what is wrong and what isn't working, we should all strive to focus on what is right.

How does it look to shift the conversation from "This is too hard" or "I can't do this!" or any other negative thought to "I am a changemaker" or "I am doing the important work." If you struggle to know if something is rooted in a negative thought, belief, or action, consider using the following phrases to help you out:

- I know I am surviving when _____.

_____

- I know I am thriving when _____.

_____

- I should _____.

_____

- I could _____.

_____

- Instead, I can _____.

_____

As we begin to shift the messages we tell ourselves from negative to positive, we also start to speak messages of affirmations to ourselves and others. Affirmations that sound something like:

- I am enough.
- I can do this important work.
- I am making a difference.
- I can listen to my body and give it what it needs.
- I am not stuck.
- I can forgive myself.
- I am worthy of rest.
- I can treat my students and myself with respect.
- I am peaceful and calm, even while doing this work.

What affirmations do you need to tell yourself? Jot down a few of your own affirmations on the next page.

A Personal Account of Building Resilience

—Regina S., elementary educator

My journey as an educator has led me from teaching rural children of poverty to urban children of wealth. For the majority of my career, I taught in urban racially diverse public schools where those economic extremes were represented in each classroom. I have never enjoyed the role of actor, presenter, or disciplinarian. I am innately a facilitator and caring adult who is there to learn from my students, and I relish the opportunity to continue as a lifelong learner. My interest in alternative education approaches stems from knowing this about my nature. I have always been more of a listener and observer than a talker. Memories of these experiences are slowly coming back to me as I move closer to retirement. Here are a few of the alternative educational approaches I learned about over the years.

With Waldorf education, I became more in touch with my need for art, music, story, and gardening. In this age of technology and distance learning, I am ever more appreciative for these opportunities. In addition, Waldorf education taught me that every student is a teacher's teacher. This is one of the reasons a teacher stays with a class throughout their elementary school years. This resonates with me as I receive the gift of each student who enters my classroom. I could never understand how a teacher could view any student as a burden, or claim that a child isn't a good fit for their classroom or their teaching style.

While teaching in a Montessori school, I became very comfortable being on the floor with small groups of children. I realized this was more suited to my nature than lecturing in front of a large class. The focus on spiritual development and a child's need for nature, beauty, peace, and routine left an indelible mark on me as an educator, parent, and soon-to-be grandparent.

I discovered the Froebel method through a parent of a Montessori student. This discovery cemented my desire to earn a master's degree with an early childhood endorsement. Being in tune with the seasons and the joy of working with young children continued to inspire me profoundly during my time of Froebel study.

Opportunity knocked once again, but this time via a magazine article about the Reggio Emilia approach. I could study this approach and earn the degree I was seeking right in my hometown! It felt like I was coming home to myself as an educator as well—a synthesis of all that inspired my early childhood educator soul.

Each of these opportunities fed a piece of my creative educator heart and brought me joy and purpose. Then suddenly and with great tension, I started feeling the exact opposite. Placed before me were high standards to achieve in order to be considered highly effective. This is a recipe for workaholism in a profession that was built on the idea that educators live and breathe to teach and nothing more. The historical notion that the school is the home of the teacher and that families give what they can in lieu of wages was all too real in my grandmother's one-room schoolhouse teaching experience. I found myself sensing that not much had changed even with a teacher's union. As a single parent, I did not have the luxury of a second income. I was on food stamps for the first five years of teaching. I couldn't afford the union perks of discounted trips to Disneyworld or various restaurants over the course of my teaching career. I still cringe when a school is referred to as "family." I am still trying to recover the lost years where my own children's needs took a back seat to the demands of my school "family."

Over time and with the passing of each year, I became more and more depleted with all of the demands on time, energy, and income. The amount of adrenaline needed to provide safety vigilance for the students and drive a curriculum with high levels of engagement, all while working to obtain test score accountability, was simply not sustainable.

Having taught in a school environment where perfectionism and workaholism ran rampant, I eventually had to learn not to care as much about what people thought of me or my teaching practice. This was challenging at first, but it became quite freeing! I still cared deeply about my role, my students, their families, and my colleagues. However, I started to say no to any demands that my inner knowing guided me away from. I reclaimed intuition for my own needs rather than waiting for someone else to help me notice and prioritize. Intuition and inspiration are at the heart of the art of teaching, but I had lost the priority of my own needs. After years of discounting myself and my individualism, I learned to own my power. I had been open to changing and learning from others, but oftentimes at my own expense.

Throughout the years of working on Sundays, constant work emails, lack of strong leadership, and perpetual exhaustion, I held on to a thread of my own nurturing by getting up at 5:30 every morning for yoga and meditation. This, along with playing music with friends once or twice a month, sustained me. The gift of debilitating sciatica at the end of a particularly hellish school year led me to seek chiropractic massages. This is the one thing I do monthly for myself, whether I can afford it or not, to prevent feeling that pain once again.

All of this led to me realizing that I needed to make some further changes. There is strong leadership with the new school I am working at, along with education truly based on relationships. And I found all of this in a traditional public school, who would've thought?! I work a very manageable 30 to 40 hours per week on a 20-hour salary. This has made a huge difference in my work/personal life balance. Within my work I am trusted and supported. I am not questioned as to why I do what I do, but what I need to do *and* what support I need. Within my personal life, I am prioritizing playing music daily and, not surprisingly, no longer struggle with tendonitis. I am also catching up with my adult children, rebuilding and strengthening relationships with them.

Interestingly enough, as a result of making these significant changes, I am not only thriving professionally but personally as well. And I've got my joy back!

Replay and Record

Our personal narratives and internal dialogues significantly impact our conversation and attitude. In fact, the stories we tell ourselves can also dictate how our body responds to situations. When our thoughts are more hopeful and positive, we send messages to the vagus nerve and activate calm within the organs and systems of the body. I highly recommend that you take time at the end of the work day to recall the day. Consider what went well, and if there were any particularly humorous or positive moments that stand out for you. Recall any moments of success that you or your students felt.

> *"If you want to find happiness, find gratitude."*
>
> —Steve Maraboli, author of *Unapologetically You: Reflections on Life and the Human Experience*

Years ago, while in the process of waiting to become a mother, I started a gratitude journal. I recorded two or three things every day that provided me with a sense of gratitude. Many people have shared the benefits of creating a practice of gratitude. According to a study in the *Journal of Personality and Social Psychology*, people who write about their gratitude show greater signs of emotional well-being.[42]

Because of the benefits of acknowledging gratitude, I began to share this practice with my students. Each year, beginning on the first of November, I ask my students to write something that they are grateful for on a Post-it note. That's right, a Post-it note! I explain that we will be engaging in this practice every day for the coming month. They always grumble and complain. We then cover the walls with their notes. Near the end of the month I ask them if they have run out of things to be grateful for and if we should stop. They always reply, without hesitation, that they still have more to share. These Post-it notes eventually fall off the wall. I don't have the heart to toss them out so instead, I turn them into little books of gratitude. I gift them to students before they leave campus for the winter holidays. They always show their appreciation by saying thank you. When they do, I remind them that this is a gift they ultimately gave themselves by engaging in a practice of gratitude!

Practicing Gratitude

Think of someone you appreciate. Close your eyes and visualize them in your mind. Think of the things they have done that give you a sense of gratitude. Picture yourself telling that person how grateful you are for them and why. Now visualize how you think they would respond to you sharing this information. How does that response make you feel? Do you notice any particular sensations or emotions? Try to find time to either share in person or in a note, why you appreciate the person you called to mind. Chances are, if you do share this information, you will feel an increased sense of happiness—and so will that person!

CHAPTER 34

TRUTHFUL STORIES

"It's important that we share our experiences with other people. Your story will heal you and your story will heal somebody else. When you tell your story, you free yourself and give other people permission to acknowledge their own story."

—Iyanla Vanzant, inspirational speaker

If, along the way, anyone has made you feel less-than or invisible, I want to tell you I am sorry. You don't need that. But, more importantly, I want to tell you that you can write a new narrative. You can be the author of your own story. Minimizing our reality and truth, or denying the struggle we experience from time to time, doesn't help us in the long run. The tendency to smother any feeling, particularly feelings of stress, discomfort, fear, or anxiety, by either ignoring or "sugar coating" them is not helpful. You are allowed to express feelings of being tired, confused, overwhelmed, sad, angry, disappointed, exhausted, worried, afraid, or stressed. This isn't to say that we should get stuck in the struggles we experience. Instead, I encourage you to experience those feelings when they arise. Give yourself some space to reflect, listen, process, and then move forward. We want to speak authentically rather than simply venting. While it feels good at the time to state whatever is upsetting us, venting excludes the practice of returning to a state of reflection to help us move forward. Eventually, we want to pivot and move, returning back toward a posture of gratitude, hope, and peace.

Say the truth about how you are doing. Tell your story. Consider writing it all down or even writing the letter to your future self with the encouragement and truth you want to offer as a reminder. The Pennebaker lab at the University of Texas at Austin found that when individuals engage in the act of translating their feelings into words, they experience emotional regulation, clarity, and a release of stress.[43] Whether it's fear of failure paralyzing us, or the worry of being portrayed as inadequate or not enough, this is never a good reason to stay silent. Stories, especially truthful stories, give the ability to understand different perspectives and practice compassion. We must have the courage to tell our own truthful story. We must practice vulnerability and trust that it is okay to not know or do everything at all times. We must know that it is okay to ask for help and to seek support when we need it. We must speak our truth. Then, let's find the movement necessary to give ourselves what we need to step forward and heal. Finally, when you are ready, you can share your story with others, who may gain a sense of connection or reprieve from your words. And, perhaps, by sharing your truthful story, you may experience even more of healing.

What Is Your Personal Story?

What is the story you need to tell?

_____

_____

_____

_____

_____

_____

_____

_____

_____

_____

_____

_____

CHAPTER 35

KEEP CULTIVATING CURIOSITY, COMPASSION, AND ACTION

*"An educator who faces challenges with
the insight that self-care is paramount
to effectiveness and therefore nurtures
oneself, is truly a resilient educator."*

—Anne G., educator

Educators are flexible and adaptable individuals. They weather the storm of constant change in the opinions of best practices, curriculum, and teacher effectiveness. They work hard to prioritize the relationships that matter the most, no matter how many angry emails or phone calls they receive, or how many crises they have to manage or avert on any given day. With the pressures and tasks continually being added on to their already-full workloads, educators are some of the most resilient people you will ever meet.

To be a resilient educator, you must know when you need to choose yourself first. It means you must know your limits and take time to care for yourself so that you can care for others. You cannot let the challenges overwhelm you or give up on yourself when it is difficult to see the benefits of what you are doing. You must build up your resources so that when another challenge occurs, you have something to draw upon and offer yourself. It means you must do whatever it takes to show up, nurture, and be present so you can get back up and move forward again, so you can move from surviving to thriving.

I long to find the exact right words to offer, so educators feel seen, heard, and acknowledged for the complexity, joy, and heaviness of the work they do. I want you to know that your struggle and suffering has not gone unnoticed. However, I also want to acknowledge that we all face struggles and hardships throughout our lifetime. The very presence of this does not mean that you are doing something wrong, but rather, it means that you are human. I don't want you to rush through moments of discomfort or despair by attempting to out run or hide from them, or even numb your way through the experience. Nor do I want you to get stuck and stay there. So, breathe deep and don't lose hope. You've got this, you can learn to become resilient so you can thrive and not just survive!

> "You may not control all the events that happen to you, but you can decide to not be reduced by them."
> —Maya Angelou

The unique journey of being an educator is a long one. I hope as you read through these pages that you found some sense of connection to those traveling along a similar path. More importantly, as you move forward, I hope you find the empowerment and liberation of caring for yourself.

The word cultivate is used to describe either preparing the land for a particular crop or in reference to acquiring or developing a particular skill. It feels like the perfect word to offer to you as you continue on this journey of moving from surviving to thriving. What "seeds" do you want to plant and tend to so they begin to take root and grow within yourself? What strengths and resources do you need to help you grow?

In order to thrive and not just survive you need to maintain a sense of curiosity, compassion, and action.

Keep cultivating curiosity. Curiosity that leads to the desire to keep learning and growing as an individual. Curiosity that cultivates learning through reading, doing, and making mistakes. Curiosity that pushes you to build your knowledge in both familiar and unfamiliar places to become even more informed. Curiosity that gives you the ability to notice the big and small things, seen and unseen. Curiosity that leads you to take the time to understand another person's story, even one that includes deep suffering, so you can respond with deeper empathy and gentleness.

Keep cultivating compassion. Compassion that leads to a shift in how you move through the world. Compassion that acknowledges adversity, shortcomings, bad days, big emotions, and struggles, and then moves you to a state of gentleness, connection, and resilience. Compassion that leads to greater acceptance and self-compassion, because ultimately, what you do for others, you do for yourself. Without compassion you become limited in the ability to offer yourself and others the care that aids in promoting and transforming physical, mental, and emotional well-being.

As Joan Halifax said, "Compassion is a necessity for our well-being, resilience, and survival." I hope you experience compassion in a way that propels you and the good of humanity forward.

Keep cultivating action. Action that leads to a transformation of not only ourselves, but to our communities as well. Action that leads to relieving stress and distress, and builds substantial capacity and empathy, rather than fatigue and burnout. Action that promotes greater regulation, sustainability, and resilience to keep moving forward regardless of whatever adversity comes your way. Action that elevates engagement, activism, and justice.

Whatever comes your way, I hope you find the courage to keep going and to increase your resiliency. I am passionate about cultivating spaces for others to slow down, pay attention, and practice compassionate courage so they can experience deeper connections. If you would like to continue the conversation, share a bit about your journey, or even your own account of how to build resilience, I would be honored to hear from you, as would Kay. My email address is below, and Kay can be reached at kay.waterson22@gmail.com.

Deep breaths, and keep rising,

SaraJane
www.risingresilient.org/risingresilient@gmail.com

REFERENCES

Aguilar, Elena. "Ride the Waves of Change." Essay. In *Onward: Cultivating Emotional Resilience in Educators*, 270–71. San Francisco: Jossey-Bass Inc., 2018.

Ansley, Brandis M., Joel Meyers, Kate McPhee, and Kris Varjas. "The Hidden Threat of Teacher Stress." TheConversation.com. August 2, 2020. https://theconversation.com/the-hidden-threat-of-teacher-stress-92676.

"Arts-Based Programs and Arts Therapies for At-Risk, Justice-Involved, and Traumatized Youths." Office of Juvenile Justice and Delinquency Prevention, May 2016, 1–9. https://www.ojjdp.gov/mpg/litreviews/Arts-based-Programs-for-Youth.pdf.

Boogren, Tina. *Take Time for You: Self-Care Action Plans for Educators*. Bloomington, IN: Solution Tree Press, 2018.

Becker, Joshua. "Minimalism Makeover." Essay. In *The Minimalist Home: A Room-by-Room Guide to a Decluttered, Refocused Life*. Colorado Springs, CO: WaterBrook Multnomah Publishing Group, 2019.

Busby, Eleanor. "Teachers Suffer More Stress than Other Workers, Study Finds." Stress.org September 22, 2019. https://www.stress.org/teachers-suffer-more-stress-than-other-workers-study-finds.

Camera, Lauren. "Sharp Nationwide Enrollment Drop in Teacher Prep Programs Cause for Alarm." USNews.com. December 3, 2019. https://www.usnews.com/news/education-news/articles/2019-12-03/sharp-nationwide-enrollment-drop-in-teacher-prep-programs-cause-for-alarm.

"Causes of Stress." *WebMD*. Accessed April 30, 2020. https://www.webmd.com/balance/guide/causes-of-stress#1.

Chamorro-Premuzic, Tomas and Derek Lusk. "The Dark Side of Resilience." *Harvard Business Review*, August 16, 2017. https://hbr.org/2017/08/the-dark-side-of-resilience.

"Childhood Trauma Is a Public Health Issue." Advisory.com. November 11, 2019. https://www.advisory.com/dailybriefing/2019/11/11/childhood-trauma.

"Chronic Stress Puts Your Health at Risk." *MayoClinic.org*. March 19, 2019. https://www.mayoclinic.org/healthy-lifestyle/stress-management/in-depth /stress/art-20046037.

Chowdhury, Madhuleena Roy. "What Is Loving-Kindness Meditation?" PositivePsychology.com. May 29, 2020. https://positivepsychology.com /loving-kindness-meditation.

"A Conversation with Seane Corn." *Conscious Life Journal.* January 3, 2018. https://myconsciouslifejournal.com/articles/interview-seane-corn.

Covey, Stephen R. *The 7 Habits of Highly Effective People: Restoring the Character Ethic.* New York: Free Press, 2004.

Drexel University. "Stress-Related Hormone Cortisol Lowers Significantly After Just 45 Minutes of Art Creation." PsyPost.org. June 15, 2016. http:// www.psypost.org/2016/06.skill-level-making-art-reduces-stress-hormone -cortisol-43362.

Emmons, Robert A. and Michael E. McCullough. "Counting Blessings versus Burdens: An Experimental Investigation of Gratitude and Subjective Well-Being in Daily Life." *Journal of Personality and Social Psychology* 84, no. 2 (February 2003): 377–89. https://pubmed.ncbi.nlm.nih.gov/12585811.

Empathy and Compassion in Society. "Interpersonal Neurobiology: Why Compassion Is Necessary for Humanity." *YouTube* video, 20:50. March 6, 2015. https://www.youtube.com/watch?v=QWE0VAzpxxg.

Forbes, Heather T. *Help for Billy: A Beyond Consequences Approach to Helping Children in the Classroom.* Boulder, CO: Beyond Consequences Institute, LLC, 2013.

"The Framework for Teaching." DanielsonGroup.org. Accessed June 27, 2020. https://danielsongroup.org/what-we-do/framework-teaching-0.

García, Emma and Elaine Weiss. "The Teacher Shortage Is Real, Large and Growing, and Worse than We Thought." *Economic Policy Institute*. March 26, 2019. https://www.epi.org/publication/the-teacher-shortage-is-real-large-and -growing-and-worse-than-we-thought-the-first-report-in-the-perfect-storm -in-the-teacher-labor-market-series.

Ginsburg, Kenneth R. *Building Resilience in Children and Teens: Giving Kids Roots and Wings.* Elk Grove Village, IL: American Academy of Pediatrics, 2011.

Halman, Paul G., Elske van de Fliert, M. Adil Khan, and Lynda Shevellar. "The Humanitarian Imperative for Education in Disaster Response." *Disaster Prevention and Management* 27, no. 2 (April 2018): 207–214. https://www.emerald.com/insight/content/doi/10.1108/DPM-10-2017-0252 /full/html.

Hanh, Thich Nhat and Katherine Weare. In *Happy Teachers Change the World: A Guide for Cultivating Mindfulness in Education*, Berkeley, CA: Parallax Press, 2017, 212.

Hammond, Zaretta. "Building the Foundation of Learning Partnerships." In *Culturally Responsive Teaching and the Brain: Promoting Authentic Engagement and Rigor among Culturally and Linguistically Diverse Students*, Thousand Oaks, CA: SAGE Publishing, 2015.

Hammond, Zaretta. "What's Culture Got to Do with It?" In *Culturally Responsive Teaching & The Brain: Promoting Authentic Engagement and Rigor Among Culturally and Linguistically Diverse Students*. Thousand Oaks, CA: SAGE Publishing, 2015.

Hanson, Rick. *Resilient: How to Grow an Unshakable Core of Calm, Strength and Happiness*. New York: Random House, 2018.

Herman, Keith C. and Wendy M. Reinke. *Stress Management for Teachers: A Proactive Guide*. New York: Guilford Press, 2015.

Herman, Keith C., Jal'Et Hickmon-Rosa, and Wendy M. Reinke. "Empirically Derived Profiles of Teacher Stress, Burnout, Self-Efficacy, and Coping and Associated Student Outcomes." *Journal of Positive Behavior Interventions* 20, no. 2 (October 6, 2017): 90–100. https://doi.org/10.1177/10983007177 32066.

Kim, Larry. "The Differences Between Busy vs. Productive People." Inc.com. February 27, 2018. https://www.inc.com/larry-kim/the-differences-between -busy-productive-people.html.

Malchiodi, Cathy A. *Creative Interventions with Traumatized Children*. New York: Guilford Press, 2015.

Maslach, Christina, Wilmar B. Schaufeli, and Michael P. Leiter. "Job Burnout," *Annual Review of Psychology* 52. (February 2001): 397–422. https://www .ncbi.nlm.nih.gov/pubmed/11148311.

Menakem, Resmaa. *My Grandmother's Hands: Racialized Trauma and the Pathway to Mending Our Hearts and Bodies*. Las Vegas, NV: Central Recovery Press, 2017.

Miller-Karas, Elaine and Kimberly R. Freeman. *Building Resilience to Trauma: The Trauma and Community Resiliency Models*. New York: Routledge, 2015.

Neff, Kristin. *Self-Compassion: The Proven Power of Being Kind to Yourself*. New York: Harper Collins Publishers, 2015.

Nhat Hanh, Thich, and Katherine Weare. *Happy Teachers Change the World: A Guide for Cultivating Mindfulness in Education*, 186–212. Berkeley, CA: Parallax Press, 2017.

Pennebaker, James W. and Janel D. Seagal. "Forming a Story: The Health Benefits of Narrative." *Journal of Clinical Psychology* 55, no. 10 (October 1999): 1243–54. https://pubmed.ncbi.nlm.nih.gov/11045774.

Perryman, Kristi, Paul Blisard, and Rochelle Moss. "Using Creative Arts in Trauma Therapy: The Neuroscience of Healing." *Journal of Mental Health Counseling* 41, no. 1 (January 2019): 80–94. https://doi.org/10.17744/mehc .41.1.07.

Pincott, Jena. "Does Grit Depend on Guts?" In *Wits Guts Grit: All-Natural Biohacks for Raising Smart, Resilient Kids*. Chicago, IL: Chicago Review Press, 2018.

Pincott, Jena. "All Is Calm, All Is Bright." In *Wits Guts Grit: All-Natural Biohacks for Raising Smart, Resilient Kids*, 226–28. Chicago, IL: Chicago Review Press, 2018.

Porges, Stephen W. *The Polyvagal Theory: Neurophysiological Foundations of Emotions, Attachment, Communication, and Self-Regulation.* First Edition. New York: W.W. Norton & Company, 2011.

Posey, Allison. *Engage the Brain: How to Design for Learning That Taps into the Power of Emotion.* Alexandria, VA: Association for Supervision and Curriculum Development, 2019.

Pranis, Kay. "Healing Circles for Teachers as a Restorative Self-Care Practice." MindfulSchools.org. December 7, 2019. https://www.mindfulschools.org /inspiration/healing-circles-for-teachers-as-a-restorative-self-care-practice.

"Preventing Adverse Childhood Experiences." Centers for Disease Control and Prevention. April 3, 2020. https://www.cdc.gov/violenceprevention/aces /fastfact.html.

Riley-Missouri, Cailin. "Lots of Teachers Are Super Stressed Out." Futurity.org. April 25, 2018. https://www.futurity.org/teachers-stress-1739832.

Sims, Sheila. "An Open Letter to All Teachers." *Medium.* December 2, 2019. https://medium.com/age-of-awareness/an-open-letter-to-all-teachers -5612e1a0338f.

Skovholt, Thomas M. and Michelle Trotter-Mathison. *The Resilient Practitioner: Burnout and Compassion Fatigue Prevention and Self-Care Strategies for the Helping Professions.* London: Routledge, 2016.

Snel, Eline. "Handling Difficult Feelings." Essay. In *Sitting Still Like a Frog: Mindfulness Exercises for Kids (and Their Parents)*, 64. Boston, MA: Shambhala Publications, 2013.

Spencer, John. "The Difference Between Being Busy and Being Productive." SpencerAuthor.com. June 26, 2018. http://www.spencerauthor.com/category/podcast/page/7.

Stronge, James H. "Qualities of Effective Teachers." In *Qualities of Effective Teachers*, 3-12. Alexandria, VA: Association for Supervision and Curriculum Development, 2018.

Strauss, Valerie. "Being Safe and Feeling Safe Aren't the Same Thing—and the Difference Will Matter to Kids When Schools Open." *The Washington Post.* July 8, 2020. https://www.washingtonpost.com/education/2020/07/08/being-safe-feeling-safe-arent-same-thing-difference-will-matter-kids-when-schools-open.

Stulberg, Brad. "Resilience Is Not About Bouncing Back. It's About Moving Forward." *Medium.* February 2, 2018. https://medium.com/personal-growth/resilience-is-not-about-bouncing-back-its-about-moving-forward-6eca35ce2f41.

"Teacher Characteristics and Trends." NCES.ed.gov. Accessed April 22, 2020. https://nces.ed.gov/fastfacts/display.asp?id=28.

Van Der Kolk, Bessel. *The Body Keeps the Score: Brain, Mind, and Body in the Healing of Trauma*. New York: Penguin Books, 2015.

"Violence Prevention." CDC.gov. April 3, 2020. https://www.cdc.gov/violenceprevention/index.html.

"Which 40 Hour Program Is Right for You?" 40HTW Landing Pages. Accessed February 16, 2020. https://join.40htw.com.

"What Is SEL?" CASEL.org. Accessed August 4, 2019. https://casel.org/what-is-sel.

"What's the Cost of Teacher Turnover?" LearningPolicyInstitute.org. September 17, 2017. https://learningpolicyinstitute.org/product/the-cost-of-teacher-turnover.

Wikipedia, The Free Encyclopedia, s.v. "Herd Mentality." Last modified September 13, 2020. https://en.wikipedia.org/wiki/Herd_mentality.

NOTES

1   Amy L. Eva and Natalie M. Thayer, "The Mindful Teacher: Translating Research into Daily Well-Being," *The Clearing House: A Journal of Educational Strategies*, Issues and Ideas 90, no. 1 (2016): 18–25, https://doi .org/10.1080/00098655.2016.1235953.

2   Eleanor Busby, "Teachers Suffer More Stress than Other Workers, Study Finds," The American Institute of Stress, September 22, 2019, https://www .stress.org/teachers-suffer-more-stress-than-other-workers-study-finds.

3   Cailin Riley-Missouri, "Lots of Teachers Are Super Stressed Out," *Futurity .org*, April 25, 2018, https://www.futurity.org/teachers-stress-1739832.

4   Eleanor Busby, "Teachers Suffer More Stress than Other Workers, Study Finds," The American Institute of Stress, September 22, 2019, https://www .stress.org/teachers-suffer-more-stress-than-other-workers-study-finds.

5   Emma García and Elaine Weiss, "The Teacher Shortage Is Real, Large and Growing, and Worse than We Thought," *Economic Policy Institute*, March 26, 2019, https://www.epi.org/publication/the-teacher-shortage-is-real-large -and-growing-and-worse-than-we-thought-the-first-report-in-the-perfect -storm-in-the-teacher-labor-market-series.

6   Lauren Camera, "Sharp Nationwide Enrollment Drop in Teacher Prep Programs Cause for Alarm," USNews.com, December 3, 2019, https://www .usnews.com/news/education-news/articles/2019-12-03/sharp -nationwide-enrollment-drop-in-teacher-prep-programs-cause-for-alarm.

7   "What's the Cost of Teacher Turnover?," Learning Policy Institute, September 17, 2017, https://learningpolicyinstitute.org/product/the-cost-of -teacher-turnover.

8   Ibid.

9   "Teacher Characteristics and Trends," NCES.ed.gov, April 22, 2020, https:// nces.ed.gov/fastfacts/display.asp?id=28.

10   Joshua Becker, "Minimalism Makeover," in *The Minimalist Home: a Room- by-Room Guide to a Decluttered, Refocused Life* (Colorado Springs: WaterBrook Multnomah Publishing Group, 2019), 9.

11   James H. Stronge, "Qualities of Effective Teachers," in *Qualities of Effective Teachers* (Alexandria, VA: Association for Supervision and Curriculum Development, 2018), 3–12.

12   "The Framework for Teaching," The Danielson Group, accessed June 27, 2020, https://danielsongroup.org/what-we-do/framework-teaching-0.

13   Stephen R. Covey, in *The 7 Habits of Highly Effective People: Powerful Lessons in Personal Change: Restoring the Character Ethic* (New York: Free Press, 2004).

14   *Wikipedia, The Free Encyclopedia*, s.v., "Herd Mentality," June 15, 2020, https://en.wikipedia.org/wiki/Herd_mentality.

15   "Which 40 Hour Program Is Right for You?" 40HTW Landing Pages, accessed February 16, 2020, https://join.40htw.com.

16   "Causes of Stress," WebMD, accessed April 30, 2020, https://www.webmd.com/balance/guide/causes-of-stress#1.

17   Keith C. Herman and Wendy M. Reinke, *Stress Management for Teachers: A Proactive Guide* (New York: Guilford Press, 2015).

18   Elaine Miller-Karas and Kimberly R. Freeman, *Building Resilience to Trauma: The Trauma and Community Resiliency Models* (New York: Routledge, 2015).

19   Brandis M. Ansley et al., "The Hidden Threat of Teacher Stress," TheConversation.com, March 2, 2018, https://theconversation.com/the-hidden-threat-of-teacher-stress-92676.

20   Christina Maslach, Wilmar B. Schaufeli, and Michael P. Leiter, "Job Burnout," *Annual Review of Psychology* 52 (February 2001): 397-422, https://www.ncbi.nlm.nih.gov/pubmed/11148311.

21   "Chronic Stress Puts Your Health at Risk," MayoClinic.org, March 19, 2019, https://www.mayoclinic.org/healthy-lifestyle/stress-management/in-depth/stress/art-20046037.

22   Paul Gerard Halman et al., "The Humanitarian Imperative for Education in Disaster Response," *Disaster Prevention and Management* 27, no. 2 (April 2018): 207–214, https://doi.org/10.1108/DPM-10-2017-0252.

23   Heather T. Forbes, *Help for Billy: A Beyond Consequences Approach to Helping Children in the Classroom* (Boulder, CO: Beyond Consequences Institute, LLC, 2013).

24   Allison Posey, *Engage the Brain: How to Design For Learning That Taps into the Power of Emotion* (Alexandria, VA: Association for Supervision and Curriculum Development, 2019).

25   "Childhood Trauma Is a Public Health Issue," Advisory.com, November 11, 2019, https://www.advisory.com/daily-briefing/2019/11/11/childhood-trauma.

26 "Preventing Adverse Childhood Experiences," Centers for Disease Control and Prevention (April 3, 2020), https://www.cdc.gov/violenceprevention/aces/fastfact.html.

27 Zaretta Hammond, "What's Culture Got to Do with It?" In *Culturally Responsive Teaching and the Brain: Promoting Authentic Engagement and Rigor among Culturally and Linguistically Diverse Students*, 33. Thousand Oaks, CA: Corwin, 2015.

28 Cathy. A. Malchiodi, Creative *Interventions with Traumatized Children* (New York: Guilford Press, 2015).

29 "Preventing Adverse Childhood Experiences," Centers for Disease Control and Prevention (April 3, 2020), https://www.cdc.gov/violence prevention/aces/fastfact.html.

30 Cathy. A. Malchiodi, *Creative Interventions with Traumatized Children* (New York: Guilford Press, 2015).

31 Tomas Chamorro-Premuzic and Derek Lusk, "The Dark Side of Resilience," *Harvard Business Review*, August 16, 2017, https://hbr.org/2017/08/the-dark-side-of-resilience.

32 Kenneth R. Ginsburg, *Building Resilience in Children and Teens: Giving Kids Roots and Wings* (Elk Grove Village, IL: American Academy of Pediatrics, 2011).

33 Dan Siegel, "Interpersonal Neurobiology: Why Compassion Is Necessary for Humanity," March 6, 2015, retrieved from https://www.youtube.com/watch?v=QWE0VAzpxxg.

34 Thich Nhat Hanh and Katherine Weare, in *Happy Teachers Change the World: a Guide for Cultivating Mindfulness in Education* (Berkeley, CA: Parallax Press, 2017), 186.

35 "What Is SEL?," CASEL.org, accessed December 4, 2019, https://casel.org/what-is-sel.

36 Eline Snel, "Handling Difficult Feelings," in *Sitting Still like a Frog: Mindfulness Exercises for Kids (and Their Parents)*, (Boston, MA: Shambhala, Publications 2013), 64.

37 Stephen W. Porges. *The Polyvagal Theory: Neurophysiological Foundations of Emotions, Attachment, Communication, and Self-Regulation*, First Edition (New York, NY: W. W. Norton & Company, 2011).

38 Jena Pincott, "All Is Calm, All Is Bright," in *Wits Guts Grit: All-Natural Biohacks for Raising Smart, Resilient Kids* (Chicago, IL: Chicago Review Press, 2018), 226–228.

39 Drexel University, "Stress-Related Hormone Cortisol Lowers Significantly After Just 45 Minutes of Art Creation," *Psypost* (June 2016),

http://www.psypost.org/2016/06/skill-level-making-art-reduces-stress
-hormone-cortisol-43362.

40   Kristin Neff, *Self-Compassion: the Proven Power of Being Kind to Yourself* (New York: William Morrow, an imprint of HarperCollinsPublishers, 2015).

41   "What Is Loving-Kindness Meditation? (Incl. 4 Scripts + YouTube Videos)," PositivePsychology.com, May 29, 2020, https://positivepsychology .com/loving-kindness-meditation.

42   Robert A. Emmons and Michael E. McCullough, "Counting Blessings versus Burdens: an Experimental Investigation of Gratitude and Subjective Well-Being in Daily Life," *Journal of Personality and Social Psychology* (U.S. National Library of Medicine, February 2003), https://pubmed.ncbi.nlm.nih .gov/12585811.

43   James W. Pennebaker and Janel D. Seagal, "Forming a Story: The Health Benefits of Narrative," *Journal of Clinical Psychology* 55, no. 10 (September 30, 1999): 1243–1254, https://doi.org/10.1002/(sici)1097-4679(199910) 55:10<3.0.co;2-n.

INDEX

W

Watson, Angela, 61

well-being of educators,

    prioritizing, 120–122

    COVID-19 pandemic, 121

windows of tolerance, 116–118

    resiliency muscles, 117

    widening, 116–118

Wits, Guts, Grit, 145

work/life balance, 36

    impact beyond classroom, 44

    work-life balancing act, 43–46

Z

zones of proximal development

    (ZPD), 54

ACKNOWLEDGMENTS

This book only exists because I have been fortunate enough to be surrounded by people who value curiosity. Having multiple people throughout the course of my lifetime show up, invest, and inspire me has kept me curious and leaning in with the hopes of gaining a better understanding and learning even more. Since my childhood, multiple educators and authors have guided me along the way and kept me dreaming that a better tomorrow was possible.

To my hundreds of students, each of you has captured my heart in some way. Whether sharing space with me in a classroom, a hallway, or some other random nook, you never hesitated to show up as your whole selves. You brought your kindness and curiosity with you again and again. You inspired me daily and filled me with hope. On the most challenging of days you offered your smiles, laughter, special notes, and hugs as a source of comfort. I write this just as much for you—you deserve the beauty of this world and so much more, and I am honored to have shared a sliver of the journey with you. Chin up, and keep going. And remember, I'm here if you need anything.

To the educators who generously gave their time, energy, passion, and guidance throughout my own personal education journey, thank you. You created for me a place that felt like I could let my guard down and feel safe. For those of you I tracked down or remained in contact with, I hope you've received my letter of gratitude and will pull it out to read again and again when you question if you've made a difference in the lives of your students. To those I have yet to reconnect with, I think of you when I am working with students, particularly during the more challenging moments, and hoping that I am guiding them with the same gentleness and wisdom you offered me.

To the many valiant educators who courageously shared their personal encounter within the world of education, I am humbled to receive your stories shared with me through both smiles and tears. I recognize the gift of being trusted with your words and your heart. I am humbled and honored to be the keeper of these stories. I hope this book reminds you of your importance. To those whose stories landed on these pages, thank you seems insufficient. You took a risk and were vulnerable. You graciously shared a glimpse into your classrooms, homes, minds, and hearts. You shared your point of view, your wisdom, and your lived experience in a transparent and authentic manner. Your stories feel like a sacred gift.

To Kay, the one who artfully brought this book to life, thank you. You not only opened up your classroom again and again, but you also opened up your heart. I have greatly appreciated seeing the world through your eyes. Your commitment to this work is what inspires me to keep going.

To the team at Ulysses Press, thank you. Thank you for valuing educators and being attuned to the complexity and demands of the job, but more importantly, the need for a hopeful message. Particular thanks go to Casie Vogel for checking in and cheering me on, especially in the days of pandemic writing and unexpected remodeling projects. Your guidance is greatly appreciated.

To my friends and family, thank you for celebrating with me when I finally had the courage to speak these words aloud. Your continued rallying and motivational messages of support filled my heart again and again. Regardless of what fills your days, I hope that you find some sense of encouragement among these pages as well. I believe that these words are just as much for you as for the educators I held in my mind while writing. Finally, I hope that I've made you proud.

And, finally, to my greatest loves and my best teachers, my partner and my children. Micah, I am grateful that all those years ago we widened the circle and welcomed one another in. Your continuous belief in me, and more importantly in this story, kept me going on even the most difficult of days. This journey of sharing life hasn't been without moments of struggle, but I am confident you would say that is where the power of transformation lies. Ultimately, we've chosen to keep showing up and loving the best we know how. When we began to pay attention, we gained a greater awareness of how to love and be loved. For that, the moments of struggle and gifts of transformation feel well worth it. To my littles, Calvin Mihretu, Elsa Meskerem, and Clarence Gemechu, who are not so little anymore, you gave me the gift of motherhood and with it taught me the beauty of "both/and" living. You have taught me that courage is often a close companion to doubt and fear, and that hurting comes right alongside healing if we make space and allow for it. You are my windows and mirrors, constantly motivating me to be a better human, and I am honored to be your student. I love you fiercely and you will have my heart always.

Kay's Acknowledgements

I would like to dedicate my contributions to this book to my mom, who taught me about bravery, empathy, and resilience.

To my brother James, who reminds me to pause, rest, and laugh.

To the brilliant SaraJane, who I could not be more proud of for sharing her truth and passion to empower educators.

And finally, to all of my students, colleagues, families, and administrators at GRCDC. Go Narwhals!

ABOUT THE AUTHOR

SaraJane Herrboldt, the founder of Rising Resilient, is a former public school teacher and district coordinator for ELD programming. With more than a decade of work in the school systems, the impact of trauma became a familiar and frequent visitor, driving her passion for promoting the well-being of others and creating opportunities that build resilience. Through coaching and professional development, she strives to create environments where individuals can slow down, get curious, and experience transformation.

She shares life with her partner, who is also an educator, along with their three greatest teachers, their children.

ABOUT THE ILLUSTRATOR

Kay Waterson is an elementary school art educator and illustrator. She received a bachelor's degree in fine art along with a K-12 teaching certification from Kendall College of Art and Design. Kay has been teaching full time for almost a decade in an urban K–5 school setting. She completed a master's degree in art education. Her thesis work, "Creativity in a Post-Traumatic Mind," explores the cognitive and emotional benefits of creative art within the process of healing from trauma. She puts the research and strategies from this body of work, which embodies her passion for art education and wellness, into practice. Additionally, Kay works part time as a freelance illustrator and painter.

Printed in the USA
CPSIA information can be obtained
at www.ICGtesting.com
CBHW050846210424
7177CB00011B/229